CREATIVE YOUTH

CREATIVE YOUTH

*How a School Environment Set Free
the Creative Spirit*

BY
HUGHES MEARNS

With a Foreword by
OTIS W. CALDWELL

and an Anthology of the High School Verse

GARDEN CITY   NEW YORK
DOUBLEDAY, DORAN & COMPANY, INC.
1931

TO

THE CLASS OF 1925

LINCOLN SCHOOL

WHO BEGAN THIS VOLUME
FIVE YEARS AGO

GRANVILLE BARKER: . . . *I remember a phrase in a little book you wrote many years ago: "We never learn anything that we did not know before."*

MOORE: *Meaning thereby that a man cannot be taught. But though he cannot be taught, he can learn, meaning thereby that he may discover a self within himself.*

—GEORGE MOORE, "Conversations in Ebury Street"

And the touch of absent-mindedness is more than any line,
Since direction counts for nothing when the gods set up a sign.

—NATHALIA CRANE, "The Janitor's Boy, and Other Poems"

FOREWORD

It has long been customary to speak of language as a vehicle for thought. This vehicular figure has too commonly been accepted as an indistinctly outlined structure on wheels, possibly moving, possibly standing still. Vehicles vary widely, however. There are heavy, jolting, rattling log wagons, freight cars, road trucks, and the noisy motorcycles; and there are noiseless bicycles, shockless motors for pleasure, health, and long-distance travel; and aeroplanes successfully inviting venturesome persons to express themselves, so to speak, by way of the air.

We cannot adequately consider this figure as applied to language without thought of the materials transferred by these vehicles. Sometimes the commodities are heavy freight in rough strong boxes, or even unpacked pieces like bars of pig iron, or heavy logs cut from strong forest trees; sometimes highly refined results of many processes of modern industry like precious chemicals, or highly polished lenses, or the fine dependable tools of modern surgery; sometimes paintings, or music, or books conveying the finest emotions of human beings. In language-conveyance as in that of public highways the vehicles are useless except as they carry appropriate and worthwhile burdens.

Too often instruction in English has devoted its time largely to construction and refinement of the means of conveying thought, and not enough to the loads to be carried. Such a procedure fails to take account of one of the truest discoveries of modern education. It is that young people best construct and refine their forms for doing their work when they are clear as to why things should be done. It isn't a question whether students may be well-trained in English, then set to work to use it, but, rather, whether they will be trained whenever the occasion for training may arise. The first method does not operate effectively; the second one does.

In the field of literature, to which this volume is devoted, certain outstanding facts may be noted as they have appeared in American education. Almost everyone believes in teaching literature to high-school pupils. Almost no one is convinced that we have succeeded in doing this with anything like satisfactory outcomes in enjoyment and appreciation of good literature. We have drilled, memorized, analyzed, dissected, and philosophized upon and within the "world's best literature." At the end we have often found our pupils examinable regarding certain standard selections, but mechanically unsympathetic with them; and there was no burning fire within driving them toward endeavors to shape their own reflections and buoyant visions into forms worthy of record in print. In literature, as in some other subjects, we have regarded pupils as learners, not prophetic doers, and have sought to instruct them, and have not tried to lead them to create. We have not really believed that all good pieces of literature are exponents of creative spirits and can be fully sensed only by those who view them from the angles of creation. We need to recognize that many, possibly most, pupils are essentially creative, but that our systems of education have forced adult standards and judgments until timidity regarding one's own writing has too often supplanted the naturally adventurous spirit of those who really wish, and very often slyly endeavor, to express themselves in verse and prose. They cannot truly enter into the world's literature except by their own endeavors to write; then in this trying, some reveal to themselves and to us the unmistakable evidences of the new writers of our own day.

For five years we have watched with fascination as a group of high-school pupils slowly have come to understand that poetry by pupils is really respectable. The shyly submitted rhyme which in bygone days, even still in many places, is falsely regarded as evidence of weak emotion is slowly assuming the dignity of real production. It may now be copied upon blackboard, discussed, improved, its rules and principles deducted almost as would be done with a demonstration in geometry or a report upon a topic in history. Furthermore, one piece of work so done serves as an opening pass key to many a door of literature which for many pupils has remained locked within library books. Literature may be and is studied objectively as is true in other school studies; it is not wholly a subjective emotional experience. But personal experience is essential to objective consideration. Then, real quality and style must work out of and not be built artificially upon the true experiences and efforts of young writers. Young people must understand that there are some well-established rules of practice. The sprightly and superficial enthusiast who wrote

Oh, Spring! Beautiful Spring!
Thou comest in the Springtime of the Year,

was merely using meaningless freedom—notwithstanding the essential correctness of the observation which she thus records. The best poems in this collection were in most cases written and many times rewritten before they reached their present form and content.

The studies herein described present the basis for a new hope for and faith in the young people of our modern day. It is usual now to hear comments about the rashness and foolhardiness of our youth. Each age has suffered this delusion regarding its youth, mistaking the true signs of progress as lack of steadfastness. Of course the new generation is different. If our memories are faithful regarding the time when we were the youth, we surely wish the new generation to be different from that of our day. Youth may try some dangerous experiments. Our generation did so. We need to recall, also, that new things, just because they are new, do not always have definite rules of procedure. This absence of adequate rules for new things must involve some measure of wastage during the period when discovery is in progress. So long as youth is essentially serious as it now is, and so long as young people really desire the good of one another as they do, even more I believe, than ever before, they are to be trusted in their thinking and in their writing. This trust must not be a half-hearted trust, but must be an actively sympathetic confidence. These youth are the next generation which shall inherit the earth.

Reading the writings which follow will surely give a large measure of new hope to all those older folk who have retained plasticity and educability.

OTIS W. CALDWELL.

CONTENTS

A SCHOOL ENVIRONMENT FOR CREATIVE WRITING

		PAGE
I.	PURPOSE	1
II.	THE CREATIVE SPIRIT STUDIED	3
III.	ILLUSTRATION OF METHOD IN CERTAIN CASES	11
IV.	HOW WE BEGAN	26
V.	THE NON-POET AND THE HALF-POEM	33
VI.	SELF-EXPRESSION THROUGHOUT THE SCHOOL	36
VII.	THE CLASSROOM ENVIRONMENT	42
VIII.	LITERARY JUDGMENT	59
IX.	CREATIVE READING	79
X.	UNSUPERVISED READING	91
XI.	THE SCHOOL LIBRARY	106
XII.	CREATIVE PROSE	110
XIII.	THE LITANIES OF YOUTH	113
XIV.	TRADITION AND THE NEXT STEP	118

LINCOLN SCHOOL VERSE, 1920–1923

(The Roman numeral after the name indicates the school grade of the writer in the year when the production was made)

SUNRISE	*Katharine Kosmak, IX*	133
BLOSSOMS	*Valerie Frankel, X*	133
PRINCESSES	*Emma Rounds, X*	134
WIND IN APRIL	*Eleanor Barnes, XI*	134
MEETING	*E. F. M., XI*	135
RED MAGNOLIAS	*Katharine Kosmak, X*	135
CITY NIGHTS	*James Flexner, VIII*	136
THE HEAD HUNTER	*William Sargent, IX*	136
THE AFTERGLOW	*Beatrice Wadhams, VII*	136

xi

PAGE

BROADWAY . . . . Tom Prideaux, IX 137
GOLD . . . . Katharine Kosmak, X 137
FIRE PICTURES . . . . . Emma Rounds, VIII 139
A SONG FOR CLEMENT MOORE . . Charlotte Bayne, IX 140
LA POINTE DU RAZ . . . . Eleanor Flexner, IX 141
THE SELF-DECEIVERS . . . . Katharine Kosmak, X 141
THE PIXIE MOMENT . . . . . Katharine Kosmak, X 142
A FLOWER REVERIE . . . Beatrice Wadhams, IX 142
DAWN . . . . Virginia Voris, IX 143
NOCTURNE . . . . James Flexner, X 143
THE WIND IS A SHEPHERD . Katharine Kosmak, VII 144
SHADOWS . . . . James Flexner, X 144
FORSYTHIA . . . . Katharine Kosmak, VIII 145
JUST BEFORE LIGHTS . . . . Beatrice Wadhams, VIII 145
DELPHINE . . . . Beatrice Wadhams, IX 146
CITY TREES AFTER SNOW . . . Emma Rounds, X 147
THE GRASPING EYE . . . Frederica P. Pisek, XII 147
HARBOR SONG . . . . E. F. M., XII 148
UP FROM UNDERSEA . . . . William Sargent, VII 149
DEEPEST MYSTERIES . . . . B. W., VIII 149
CURED: A BEDSIDE POEM . . . . . . E. F., IX 150
IN THE HOURS OF DARKNESS . . James Flexner, IX 151
WIND OF DAWN . . . . . Wynne Fairfield, XII 152
PHANTOMS . . . . Emma Rounds, VIII 152
THE OPIUM EATER . . . . . Tom Prideaux, IX 153
SKIP-SCOOP-ANELLIE . . . . The Lincoln Imp. IX 154
POOR PUSSY-WILLOWS . . . . Pixie Rain, IX 154
THE SPOILERS . . . . . . Emma Rounds, IX 155
THE BALLAD OF A PHILOSOPHER'S PICNIC. . J. F., X 155
ON HIS KINDNESS . . . . . Paul M. Herzog, XI 156
ON THE IMITATIONS OF WORDSWORTH IN EARLY CHILDHOOD
                                Emma Rounds, X 157
THE DOOR STANDS OPEN . . . Wynne Fairfield, XII 158

LINCOLN SCHOOL VERSE, 1923–1925

PRELUDE . . . . Ella Fohs, XI 164
SPRING VENDERS . . . . . Tom Prideaux, X 164
WILDFLOWER . . . . . . Beatrice Wadhams, XI 164

CONTENTS

MOON MADNESS . . . . *Zara Moxham, X* 165
INTIMATIONS . . . . *Philip Jordan, XII* 166
DOWN THE NIGHTS AND DOWN THE DAYS
                                  James Flexner, XI 166
THE PATH . . . . *Alwin Pappenheimer, XI* 168
ABSENCE. . . . . *Virginia Voris, XI* 168
THE POOL OF LILITH . . . . . *Philip Jordan, XII* 168
FIRST SNOW . . . . *Beatrice Wadhams, XII* 170
OH, SHEPHERD . . . . *Margaret Mayo, VII* 170
TWILIGHT . . . . *Eleanor Barnes, XII* 171
WEARY OF MYSELF . . . . . . *Louise Laidlaw, XI* 171
TO TIMMY . . . . *E. B., XII* 171
WILDA . . . . *Beatrice Wadhams, XI* 171
CLOCKMAKER'S SONG . . . *Katharine Kosmak, XII* 173
OUR MOON . . . . . *Louise Burton Laidlaw, XII* 173
PATHS . . . . *E. B., XII* 174
THREE POEMS . . . . *Dorothy Rand, XII* 175
YOUTH'S EYES . . . . *Zara Moxham, X* 176
YOU STAND ON A MOUNTAIN . *Katharine Kosmak, XI* 176
IN A RAILWAY STATION . . . . *Eleanor Barnes, XII* 178
GREEN JANUARY . . . . . *Katharine Kosmak, XI* 179
THE EGOTIST IN HIS ORCHARD . . *Tom Prideaux, XI* 180
SOME AND OTHERS AT THE PRIVATE VIEW
                                  Philip Jordan, XII 180
QUASSIA WOOD . . . . . . *Arthur Bullowa, XI* 180
FRENCH MINUET . . . . . *Beatrice Wadhams, XII* 181
THE SUN-SHUNNER . . . . . *Tom Prideaux, XI* 182
FIREWORKS . . . . *Tom Prideaux, XI* 182
DECEMBER . . . . . *Sanderson Vanderbilt, XI* 183
NATURE NOTES . . . . . . *Emma Rounds, XI* 183
TO JULIA, CAUTIONING HER AGAINST INFECTIOUS DISEASES
                                  Emma Rounds, XI 184
THE CIRCUS . . . . *Tom Prideaux, X* 184
THE MORON TURNS . . . . . *Emma Rounds, XI* 186
TROPICS . . . . *Tom Prideaux, X* 187
MORAL TALES . . . . . . *Emma Rounds, XI* 189
ON MY LADY'S FINGERNAIL . . *Hope Spingarn, XII* 190
URBAN TRANSPORTATION SONGS . *Emma Rounds, XI* 190

PAGE

He Did! . . . . Pauline Baerwald, VIII 191

Moon . . . . Tom Prideaux, X 192

Out There . . . . Stephen Duggan, XI 192

The Beauty of Her . . . . Alice Habberton, XI 193

Tang. . . . . Zora Head, XI 193

Seasonal Impressions . . . . Lincoln Reis, XI 193

Kin . . . . Ella Fohs, XI 194

The North Wind. . . . . Lincoln Reis, XI 194

The Land of Things Forgotten

Anne Pappenheimer, VIII 195

The Call of the Air . . . Gholson Kittredge, VIII 195

Tired Water . . . . . Anne Pappenheimer, VIII 196

Tinsel . . . . Beatrice Wadhams, XII 197

Cavalier's Ditty . . . . . Aline Wechsler, IX 197

Sea-Gods . . . . . . Wilma Roelofsma, XI 198

Akib, King of Egypt's Son . . Samuel Lynch, IX 198

Rain-Riding . . . . . . Mary Rumely, VII 200

Song . . . . Beatrice Wadhams, XII 201

O Sailors! . . . . Aline Wechsler, IX 201

Lullaby. . . . . . . Priscilla Wadhams, VIII 202

The Blackfeet of Montana . . William Sargent, IX 202

Some Day, Maybe . . . Priscilla Wadhams, VIII 204

Oh, Fishman, Sweet Fishman . . John Croly, VIII 204

New Years . . . . . . Susan Kronthal, IX 205

Morning . . . . . . Nathalie Swan, VII 205

Piteous Eyes . . . . . . Mary Spurrier, VIII 205

The Barn-Swallow . . . . William Sargent, XI 206

Bizarre . . . . . Anne Pappenheimer, VIII 206

Our Lady of the Shipwrecked . Eleanor Flexner, X 207

People . . . . Philip Jordan, XI 207

We Meet Again . . . . . Tom Prideaux, XI 208

Anchorite . . . . . . Sanderson Vanderbilt, XI 208

On Certain Poets . . . . Katharine Kosmak, XI 209

Coquette . . . . Zora Head, XI 212

Sophomore . . . . Zora Head, XI 212

At Kenilworth . . . . . Louise Laidlaw, XII 212

Those Things That Once Have Brought Us Happiness

Arthur E. Bestor, Jr., XI 213

CONTENTS

The Galley-Proof of the Poetic Pudding

                             Emma Rounds, XI 213

Plane Geometry . . . . Emma Rounds, XI 214

Honors . . . . Philip Jordan, XII 215

Walt Whitman . . . . . . Lincoln Reis, XI 215

Jazz, Tinter of Souls . . . James Flexner, XI 216

Lincoln . . . . Aline Wechsler, IX 219

Content on a Bus . . . . . Zara Moxham, XI 219

Lanterns . . . . . . Sanderson Vanderbilt, XI 220

Christmas After Thanksgiving Katharine Kosmak, XI 220

When I Was Very Young . Katharine Kosmak, XII 220

Explanations . . . . Nancy Dennett, XI 221

Confessional . . . . . . Philip Jordan, XII 221

Ah! . . . . Wilma Roelofsma, XI 222

Patient . . . . Ella Fohs, XI 223

Well! . . . . Wilma Roelofsma, XI 223

Vital . . . . Charles Liebman, Jr., XI 223

Sprig . . . . Sanderson Vanderbilt, XI 224

Succour . . . . Arthur Bullowa, XI 224

A Ballad of Lady Moon . . Aline Wechsler, IX 225

The Hills . . . . William Sargent, XI 225

The Dark Hours of the Night . Zara Moxham, XI 226

Fool . . . . Wilma Roelofsma, XI 227

Queen of the Pond . . . Sanderson Vanderbilt, XI 227

Vendetta . . . . Zora Head, XI 228

Wind-Wolves . . . . . . William Sargent, XI 228

Now . . . . Arthur E. Bestor, Jr., XI 229

The Four-Master . . . . . Philip Jordan, XII 230

Beyond . . . . James Flexner, XI 230

Heaven . . . . Anne Pappenheimer, IX 231

Two Sonnets on the Theatre . Tom Prideaux, XI 232

Prayer . . . . James Flexner, XII 233

Horizontal. . . . . . . Tom Prideaux, XI 233

So Long . . . . James Flexner, XII 234

A SCHOOL ENVIRONMENT
FOR
CREATIVE WRITING

CREATIVE YOUTH

I. PURPOSE

JUDGES have assured us that the poems in this volume have merit. When a portion of Tom Prideaux's *Circus*[1] was read before the New York Art Club at one of its annual Authors' Nights, William Rose Benét shouldered through the audience to demand further particulars about the poet and to read for himself the description of the acrobats in glittering regalia careening at their dizzy heights "like birds among the jungles of a dream." Amid the clamor of voices all about us he read the concluding lines:

> Then bowing when their lauded act is ended
> And tossing kisses, jaunty and so glib,
> I wonder if they really comprehended
> They've tickled Death along his bony rib!

"That makes the small hairs rise on the back of my neck," he said warmly; "and I always know it's a good poem when the small hairs rise on the back of my neck!" If Professor William Lyon Phelps had been present he might have offered the test of "that unmistakable spinal chill" which first announces to him a bit of literary art.

Our own sure sign is a rush of animation that sets us chattering and gesticulating, like the sudden loosening effect of the wine of yesteryear. Without admitting the value of these æsthetic criteria, we have evidence from many sources that this group of poems by high-school pupils has attracted more than usual attention. As the verses appeared month

---

[1]See page 184.

by month in the school magazine, *Lincoln Lore*, recognition of their interesting quality came from all sides: from college classes, from editors and professors, from parents, from children in other schools, and from teachers and educational administrators generally. In two years the magazine was included in that select list *The Yearbook of American Poetry;* but perhaps the crowning recognition was the selection of a *Lincoln Lore* poem for publication in Braithwaite's *Anthology*,[1] an honor that for poets has come to take on something of the nature of an annual national award. With that poem *Sunrise*, by Katharine Kosmak, we appropriately opened our first collection of Lincoln School verse and prose,[2] the poetic portion of which we republish here as Part I of the anthology.

It interests us, of course, that the work of these high-school students should have been received so well and that some of their poems should have been considered worthy of a place among the best contemporary American poetry, but our object has never been to produce the exceptional. We are not primarily interested in making poets or even in making writers;[3] our purpose has been simply to set up such an environment as might extend further the possibilities in creative writing of pupils of high-school age. We had faith that the productive range is more extensive than commonly believed, and that the best literary education comes with the amplest self-realization of the individual at whatever age he happens to be. So we have not thwarted effort, but encouraged it, rather; we have treated with respect every sort of genuine self-expression, and have rigorously refrained from a too pedagogic correction.

---

[1] *An Anthology of Magazine Verse for 1922*, ed. William Stanley Braithwaite (Small, Maynard).

[2] *Lincoln Verse, Story, and Essay* (First Series) (The Lincoln School of Teachers College, New York City, 1923).

[3] "And do many of your children go in for Art afterwards?" we queried. "Not as a rule. They go into all sorts of professions and trades. That's quite right—that's what I like. I like to think of Art coloring all departments of life rather than being a separate profession." From *The Child as Artist, Some Conversations with Professor Cizek*, by F. M. W., 1921, distributed by the Art Alliance, New York City.

Our educational aim has been put most satisfactorily by William Stanley Braithwaite, one of the earliest to appreciate the significance of the work of these young writers:

It is wonderful material you have to work with [he writes], the imaginative, elemental substances of the youthful mind. It is the time when, if they are guided, they can come under those influences which lead to the secrets in the heart of man and nature. Once made really to see *and* feel these secrets, they seldom lose the power and significance of them; and even if they do not become expressed poets later on, they will become possessed of that culture whose spirit is poetry. It will be wonderful later [he added], to look back and see what perfection has been created "either in manifest art or manifest personality."

II. THE CREATIVE SPIRIT STUDIED

THE attitude of the artist toward his work has been an unfailing theme of classroom interest, and in this connection we have never drawn any sharp distinction between fine arts and letters. From the point of view of the Creative Spirit, the arts are one; only the product is different. Constantly, as here and there the excellent verse appeared, the informal talk has centered around the mystery of the product of the artist. Almost any one of our pupils could now discuss the matter from personal experience: deep within us is a vast imaginative power, varying in quality and in intensity but probably the same in each of us; it finds for itself, in devious unreasonable ways, an artistic expression. This point of view could not be really alive among pupils unless they recognized it as a true interpretation of their daily experience. We ask ourselves—I am now presenting one of our methods of approach—how thoughts come to us; where we got this and that fine idea, this felicitous phrase, that stimulating picture or figure of speech; and while we never achieve completely satisfying answers, we learn to respect the instinctive self within us, that possible product of animal and spiritual race-accumulations which is, at its best, so right and sure, so beautiful and wise. The large liberty permitted us in our school, we comprehend eventually, is to set more free that sure, right, beautiful, and wise self.

Everyone is conscious of the curious personal phenomena, not easily explained, by which art comes into being. It is accompanied by elation, by an almost unnatural feeling of well-being; fatigue disappears; enormous quantities of labor can be accomplished; one can work for hours without a demand for rest, or even for food or sleep. Young people know all about this characteristic of the vital energy; their lives are rich in the experience of its ways; therefore they can talk about it with understanding. Long ago I ceased taking notes on casual remarks of this and that pupil, as we talked of his writing. The proof is clear to me that in this respect pupils do not differ from adults, except, I am sure, that children are in the main still artists, while adults have too often ceased to be.

Here are some excerpts: "I stayed up nearly all night to do that. Mother came in and found me at five o'clock dressed and the light lit. I pretended to be asleep at my desk, but I was more awake than daytime." "I wrote that notebook full and didn't eat or anything. Terrible hungry after it was done. Thought I was sick, maybe. Wasn't hungry"—pointing to the book—"then, though." "Everybody else was shivering with the cold, and I was sitting over in the corner working at this, and thought it was fine, and had my coat unbuttoned, too." Besides these, I have the instances of two boys, both of the highest scholastic standing, who cut school in order to get consecutive hours of steady, uninterrupted work at the thing that had gripped them beyond the powers of resistance. The result in one case is a scientific paper which has been much spoken of as superior to high college standard; the result in the other case is one of the best poems in this collection.

Mothers are first to be aware of this grip of inspiration

From them I have two types of returns, one in which the mother rejoices that her boy (or girl, of course) is at so self-absorbing a task; the other from the sort who, having scheduled their children to a time table which takes care of every minute of the day and night, object to anything "irregular"—by which they mean any stepping outside the path predestined by them.

Early we find out that something interferes—many things. Shame is one of them, the result, frequently, of the false standards of our mates and of our elders. A laugh, goes the saying, is as good as a criticism; a laugh may seal forever one outlet of the spirit. Genius, of course, rises above such limitation; but I hope it is understood that the question has here nothing to do with genius but simply with young persons of high-school age.

Coercion, it is generally agreed, destroys, although many pupils insist that their best work has been produced under the terrible compulsion of necessity. The approach of the time of printing the school magazine has driven the editors to a levy upon contributors for copy which has often led to a half-the-night struggle to produce; but out of this artificial and really hateful tasking have come some astonishing revelations of the inner self. Many of the poems in this volume are the results of self-imposed tasks, a deliberate setting oneself to work for real or fancied needs. As a rule, however, the creative spirit may not be driven out, but it may be enticed out. In fact, it seems to have many of the qualities of Poe's Imp of the Perverse, an incorrigible obstinacy that lays itself out to defeat those who would arbitrarily command it. An illustration of this point I take from my notes of cases: The Director of the School tells of meeting the author of *Moon Madness*[1] just after the appearance of this, her first published poem, had brought her the acclaim of pupils and teachers alike. "Now," he said, curious to see how she

<hr>

[1]Page 165.

would react, "I want you to write me a poem, and I shall give you the subject"—he then gave it to her—"and its length—about so long," he measured; "and I want it done for a meeting of junior high-school pupils to-morrow afternoon. There will be no objection if it is humorous." "But, Doctor Caldwell," she exclaimed, astonished at the order, "poems are not written that way! They come because of the way I think and feel *myself*. I will try to write one for you, of course, but I don't think it will be the one you want, for I don't know even myself what it is going to be; but it must be my own, and when you tell me what to write about—that, I'm afraid, will make me not want to write it at all, because it wouldn't be mine, you see, but—" pathetically desirous of not offending—"but yours, if you see what I mean." He saw exactly that she understood and was glad.

We discover, too, what seems to be a law of the creative spirit, that it does not, except on rare occasions, give forth its best at once. The sad part of the mystery of creative effort is that with every sign of the divine afflatus the product is not always good. Here is where a sympathetic understanding of the forces at work is imperatively needed from teacher or friend (I wish there could be no real distinction!). Out of the mass of not-so-good may come enough material to build on; or, at least, some obstruction to the Creative Spirit is got out of the way. Inferior work seems sometimes to appear of necessity before the deeper best may reach expression. All good things must first be worked over, therefore; and if our first rough drafts are a little ridiculous, we learn early not to be discouraged. Particularly we fight against the self-disgust that would destroy those first attempts. If we have any arbitrary rule it is, "Never destroy a scrap, no matter how bad it may seem to be." The figure that has been most instructive here is that of a new stream, muddied, at first, until the water from the far spring begins to flow. A more practical illustration comes from the painter: he makes no outright perfect canvases; his failure is so constant that he accepts it calmly as a natural step toward that best which, if he persists, will appear in its own good time.

The painter's experiences come up often in the daily discussions of our art; so it was natural that from the pupils I should hear first of the traveling exhibition of paintings, drawings, and woodcuts made by the children taught by Professor Cizek in his classes at the Vienna School of Arts and Crafts; and that the members of our classes should go there voluntarily in groups and singly to study an art so allied to their own, particularly as it was done by children of almost exactly their own age. Reproductions of the paintings and woodcuts of these Austrian children soon appeared on the classroom bulletin board. One pupil brought the descriptive pamphlet, *The Child as Artist*;[1] it was passed around until all had read it. A boy remarked, with an amused glance at the teacher, it must be admitted, "Now I shall know what to say to people when they ask me about the poetry of the Lincoln School. I shall read them this:

"How do you do it?" we asked at last, when we had looked at some hundreds of the productions of Professor Cizek's pupils each more delightful and original than the last.

"But I don't do it," he protested with a kind of weary pity for our lack of understanding. "I take off the lid, and other art masters clap the lid on—that is the only difference."

Writing men, I often remind them, tell the same story of those monstrous first appearances before the final draft reveals something approaching the hoped-for result. We bring to our discussions first-hand information from these men. From every side comes the story of scribbled notes,

[1]The same title is used to introduce an excellently illustrated article on the work of Professor Cizek's children in the *Independent*, December 20, 1924.

often disjointed and sprawling; of rewritings; of eliminations
and scribbled additions; of more rewritings; of later reshap-
ings of the whole, new balancings, better proportionings; and
of a final reconsideration of each part for its effect upon the
reader.   And after that, when the creative fire has spent
itself, the mechanical editing into a properly spelled, punctuated, paragraphed piece, matters which the schoolroom is
prone to put as the first and only consideration.   In its place
it is of high importance, this coldly intellectual stage; the
value of a piece of created work is raised there in direct proportion to the intelligence of the creator.

We note early that form is not the first consideration.
First is the idea, or, perhaps, merely the vague but insistent
feeling to compose—"the itch to write," the wise ancients
called it.   I tell them of Santayana's remark to a group of
his students that for him it was often simply the irrepressible
urge to put something-he-knew-not-what down upon a piece
of blank paper, although he said he got to expect from past
performances that a poem was about to emerge; that, frequently, the end came forth briskly before the beginning, or
it might turn out to be the middle, after all; and that, likely
as not, he might have for his pains nothing but an unintel-
ligible fragment, which, if he was patient and waited, would
grow its necessary and seemingly predestined parts.   "Inspiration" is the word we used to call this natural phase of
creative work, as if a mediumistic "control" were guiding the
result.   Indeed, the product at its best has many of the qualities that suggest the impulse of an alien but friendly spirit.

However, we do not wait for inspiration; we know that it
comes quicker if we go out to meet it.   Having a special place
in which to work, and always using that place, is a good way for
many; and to go there often with paper and pencil, making
a regular rendezvous with inspiration, as it were.   There,
initial distaste for working may often slip into a sudden rush
of desire.   We go to the accustomed place, locking out all

tempting outside opposition—even the view!—and wait. It doesn't matter if sometimes we spend the time making iterated sketches of the same type of profile; or if the paper becomes a blotch of formless inky design. Sometimes we write the flattest stuff for half the time; then, without our even knowing it, the Silent Doors slide, and we are in the Never Never Land. Stevenson tells of watching the workmanlike painters at Barbizon. "My job is like theirs," he cried. "Every day they go at their work, their job, not waiting for inspiration or mood or even for subject. Something, a little, every day; and the result is mountainous!" We know that this picture remained with him the remainder of his days, a rebuke to bad writing habits, and a stimulus for his duller hours.

Of course, none of us has the same mental make-up, so there is no sure recipe for enticing the creative forces to work; the point for the pupil is by studying himself to find out what for him is best.

And to make sure lest our elders may think that the creative impulse is a wild and turbulent thing, we hasten to add that an outward calmness is one of its chief characteristics. It flows along like Arnold's hidden river in *Buried Life;* it can be there in the midst of absorbing play and wordy debate, consciously there, waiting for its right moment of isolation; it can operate in the very madding crowd and no one but the owner be aware of its existence. For Shelley is right in claiming, in his *Defence of Poetry,* that the poetic fire is at its height long before the comparatively cool business of putting it to words on paper. This is why teachers, parents, and friends fail so often to note its presence. Our five-year experiment in creative writing, if it does nothing else, should prove the worth of watching a little more keenly for its many and varied sensitive manifestations.

The formal side is important, we know; but experience in the making of imaginative verse and prose leads us to the

conclusion that it does not come first in importance. They
have their places, grammar, rhetoric, the principles of
composition, rhyme schemes, climax, speed, *dénouement*,
impasse—one might go on until all the textbook categories
have been listed; but to the artist all these take meaning only
because of their recognition as part of the inner reality of
thought and feeling.[1] The schools not only place them first
in the business of instruction, but offer traditionally little
else. Definition and classification, important tools of
scholarship, have an ancient right to priority. One remembers St. Chrysostom's reply to those who would cate-
chize him with definitions as a test of his piety, "I had
rather *be* contrite than skilled in the definition thereof."

Recently Willa Cather asked a group of us, all teachers
of English, why the formal side of literature was stressed
in the school at the expense of the sole reason for its value,
namely, its effect upon the mind and spirit of man. The
answer was, first, the recognition of the formal side of literature—its shape, arrangement, and organization—is the
easier to teach; and, second, we teachers do not seem to know
anything else. While the discussion with Miss Cather
brought out that teachers and grammarians are rarely themselves artists, we contended, in our defense, that a feeling
of this lack had already reached the elementary school,
where amendment in method and material was undergoing
notable changes; and we cited the colleges that were beginning to question the purely formal and historical approach,
as instanced in recent appointments of poets like Witter
Bynner, Robert Frost, Percy Mackaye, Robert Bridges.
The artist has been more conspicuous in the college, perhaps,
than in any other rank of teachers. Longfellow and Holmes

---

[1] "I shifted the little pens of color about, laid one color against the other. . . . Suddenly there had flashed into my consciousness, for perhaps the first time in my life, the secret inner world of the painters. . . . The true painter revealed all of himself in every stroke of his brush. . . . Very well, then, the words used by the tale-teller were as the colors used by the painter. Form was another matter. It grew out of the materials of the tale and the teller's reaction to them. It was the tale trying to take form that kicked about inside the tale-teller at night when he wanted to sleep."—Sherwood Anderson in *A Story Teller's Story* (Huebsch, 1924).

set traditions in this country, if not by their teaching, then by their acknowledged fame as literary artists. Professor Baker's "Workshop 47" was one of the notable attempts to meet understandingly the needs of the creative writer. Brander Matthews, Bliss Perry, William Vaughn Moody, Robert Herrick, John Erskine, Katharine Lee Bates, Grace Hazard Conkling, Stark Young, David Morton, Alfred Noyes, to stop short in a long list, are teachers who have added to scholarship a perception, through participation, of the unique travail of the "maker" in letters. Evidence could be found, however, that often the artist has even here found himself opposed by the large number of formalists on the staff.[1]

III. ILLUSTRATION OF METHOD IN CERTAIN CASES

ONE sure sign of the genuineness of any art product is its unique character. Art never repeats and never copies. That the creative spirit has expressed itself among these pupils is evidenced by the individual note. Few echoes of other poets' poetry are here, except where the imitation is obviously intended, but even in parody the individuality of the performance marks the verse as an original. As Braithwaite put it, we are seeking "the imaginative, elemental substances of the youthful mind"; when these have appeared we have made much of them; when the hackneyed copy was offered we labeled it as such without enthusiasm. Consequently, such traditional poetic tags as *wilst, ere, o'er, fain would, forsooth, alack, O thou*, and the like, were soon taboo; along with traditional poetic ideas concerning the sun, moon, and stars, birds (nightingales, larks, and cuckoos in American landscapes!), and those flowers that bloom in the spring,

[1] "In creative circles it is regarded as singular that Robert Frost intermittently and Robert Herrick persistently hold professorships; in professional circles it is commonly thought best, when an active poet or novelist is added to the staff of a university, to keep them below the salt with the instructors or among the side shows with the extension lecturers."—Carl Van Doren in *Many Minds*, the chapter called "The Great Tradition."
  ʙynner hints ("On Teaching the Young Laurel to Shoot," *New Republic*, Dec. 5, 1923, Part II) that some of the "active poets" were not reappointed in one university when it was discovered that they lacked the doctor's degree!

which, according to an excellent poetic authority, have nothing to do with the case.

> Triolets, villanelles, rondels, rondeaus,
> Ballads by the score with the same old thought.

Went also rhymes for rhyme's sake, as well as the lazy *do* put in to round out a short line, and all the "faint iambics" of Petit the Poet.

Our first really exceptional poem came near the end of the first year of this experiment. The writing of verse had already begun to have a serious place in the work of the school, so a casual suggestion to the graduating class that a "class poem" might be appropriate brought a lengthy "poem" which featured the commonest of class-poem symbolism, the ships that set sail on uncharted seas, some of which would be wrecked on the rocks, others lost in storms and never traced, others that would reach the farther shore. There were side references, too, to the rungs of ladders and unexplored mountain paths. This was the more remarkable as it was the product of a girl of rare originality of mind, and, in music, an accepted artist. The stanzas contained one provocative line, however, the first,

> The ever-passing steps went by our door.

She handed it to me with a smile and as I read watched me with what I conceived to be a well-assumed indifference. I folded it slowly and said nothing. "Will it do?" she asked.

Obviously she had worked seriously and long. Should one risk the danger of discouraging effort? The mysterious forces of the spirit are notably sensitive to criticism.[1] With a younger pupil I should have placed the manuscript carefully in my pocket with a non-committal remark, and have

---

[1] "It was very little more than one hundred years ago—one hundred and five, to be exact—that Keats seriously pondered whether he should not give up poetry, and use the few pounds that remained to him in qualifying as a physician in Edinburgh. . . . *The Quarterly* had just killed 'Endymion,' pole-axed it; . . . the knocking on the head forever of his chance of becoming a successful poet had its effect upon him. Such things do."—John Middleton Murry in "Some Thoughts on Criticism," *Literary Review*, Dec. 13, 1924.

waited until it was forgotten. In this case I banked heavily upon the intelligence before me and said, "No; it's very bad."

"What's wrong with it?" she came back aflame.

"Why do people do it?" I parried. "Every high-school senior class has at this moment one or a dozen persons busy on this sort of thing. And they will all turn out the same product, as if it were a standardized graduation article, as like as—as like as college alma mater songs, and almost as bad." Then I went abruptly into details and shamelessly exposed the commonplaceness of her work—she whose mind, I knew, had ever disdained the commonplace!

"But your first line!" I spoke with sudden enthusiasm. "That really startled and waylaid me. That first line is the poetry of our time. The rest is hopelessly trade-marked."

She asked, with a touch, I suspected, of irony, about "the poetry of our time." But I knew she was interested. That one crumb of comfort, the single worthy line, had caught her.

In a swift sketch, as the class was assembling, I told her of the method of the modern poets, how they had boldly discarded all the "poetic phrases" and "poetic thoughts" of the past and had made fresh formulæ of word and idea to match their own observed world. Briefly I touched the main points in the credo of the new poetry.

Without a word of reply she left me abruptly to take a seat at the back of the room.

During the period a girl came forward to say quietly, "You'd better let her go. She says she can't stand it here much longer."

"Do tell her to go," I whispered back. I had failed in my attack, I thought; I had been too direct.

She went out of the room with her eyes set at a strange focus, far away. Chairs and small tables were thrust aside roughly; the door was slammed open. But she heard neither that, she claimed later, nor the laugh of the class; and had no remembrance of a precipitous exit. Her friend volunteered as an apology, "She said she had a poem in her, and that if she had to stay in this room another minute without writing it she would scream."

Before the hour was over she brought back the astonishing lines of *The Door Stands Open*.[1] They came from her in a torrent, with hardly the necessity of an erasure. Nothing remained of the original verses but the first line.

I have read the poem often to groups of parents and teachers. It never fails to make a penetrating impression. The wonder is how a girl of her inexperience could know intuitively so much about life. The pathos of futile scholarship is in the lines,

> There stands a man who watches those who start out;
> He sees them drop unnoticed things of value
> For which he stoops and searches in the dust;
> He is one who went out and has returned
> With nothing.

The blight of ignorance has touched this blithe figure:

> Here returns a man whose face must once have been like that
>   youth's;
> His eyes are broken windows, and he babbles without sense.

Commenting upon this curiously true insight, Professor Franklin Baker said:

They know before they know, these children. They foresee experience before they have experience. In some respects they are wiser as children than ever they will be later.[2]

---

[1] Page 158.

[2] The best brief account of the point of view of contemporary poetry is in the Preface to Untermeyer's *Modern American Poetry*, revised edition (Harcourt, 1921), which includes Amy Lowell's six articles of faith of the Imagists. A critique of these articles in Professor Erskine's *The Kinds of Poetry* (Duffield, 1920) must not be missed; his important chapter, "The New Poetry," contains a passage that sums up all the counsel a teacher ever need aspire to give to young poets: "Acquire new cadences, the imagists advise us, so that you may express a new idea; yet if we have the new idea and try to give it sincere expression, it is hard to see how we shall miss a new rhythm—the excellence of Mr. Masters and of Mr. Frost is that they have built their art from the inside outward, and their success illustrates once more, what the young poet will not easily learn, that a large audience waits for those whose heart and mind compel them to speak."

A boy permits me to tell the story of his earliest efforts, how he brought me a small volume of verses that were like *The Young Visiters*, so bad that they were good. The war had made a terrible impression upon him; he wrote of battle and blood with a seriousness that was almost comic.

My advice was to keep them one year, and then to show them to me. I forget now how I made that suggestion reasonable without offense. I told him to keep on writing, however. Then one day he gave me

CITY NIGHTS

When the lights of the city are bright and they gleam,
  And the moon looks down on the level street,
I always dream the selfsame dream
Of hills that are wide and of woods that are green
  And of places where two brooks meet.

Since then he has moved forward steadily, with never a trace of his former Ashfordisms. A considerable body of commendable verse he has already achieved, most of which is republished here; *Down the Nights and Down the Days* and *Beyond*,[1] we venture to believe, are the work of an authentic poet.

In the illustrations used so far, two points stand out that might be helpful to teachers and parents: first, that when the way is made easy, poetry is brought to us good and bad. That means, simply, that poetry is already there. Much of it has already been written, is bound away in secret note-books or hoarded in private drawers. Evidence of this is overwhelming. At the beginning, after we had won the confidence of those who had already written, we found veritable volumes, the chirography showing grades of script from the earliest gross lettering to the latest ill-spelled scrawl. And even before that, doubtless, the young authors had

---

[1] Pages 166 and 230.

lisped in numbers![1] Evidently poetic expression is one of our primal instincts, a useful thing in the barbarous days when rhythmic dancing and singing were serious open-air occupations of adults; it atrophies with disuse, for we do not notice among the serious street occupations of our adult citizenry any widespresd attempts to "dance the juba from wall to wall." We are in this respect like the house dog that James used to love to talk about, who sought to bury his bone under a rug; one remembers that James's dog gave up burying bones in the house after he found the sure daily meat in his dish.

The second point is that the poetic insight once really obtained—one must forget the dog parable now—is never again lost; or, as Mr. Braithwaite so finely put it, "Once made to really see *and* feel the secrets, they seldom lose the power and significance of them."

There should be a third point here on method: no matter how bad the product may be, the poet must be invited to do more. "Very interesting," you say; "very interesting, indeed! Now you let me have this for my collection, but keep on writing. This is what we call personal poetry; it is excellent, for you and for me, who understand it; but it isn't the kind that strangers would instantly like. Some day you will write a poem as true and as sincere and as honest as this one, and every reader will feel exactly as you do about it. And there is only one way to write that sort of poem, the way you have written this one, fearlessly, carelessly, a bit of your-own-feeling, nobody-else's. All good poetry is first 'personal poetry' and then 'everybody's poetry.'"

But this already gives a wrong impression of the part the teacher plays in criticism. Consider that the writing of

---

[1] "Nathalia had been writing her verse for several months before Mr. and Mrs. Crane came across it, writing it without fuss or excitement and storing it in a small and private album, content apparently with the record of whatever pleasure the rereading of it gave her. If she had, even secretly, any concern with such vanity as applause, she certainly did not betray it."— *Nathalia at Ten*, by Nonnally Johnson in introduction to *The Janitor's Boy and Other Poems*, by Nathalia Crane (Seltzer, 1924).

LINCOLN LORE

JANUARY 1924

People	Philip Jordan
The Black Hills	Aileen Gould
Our Lady of the Shipwreck	Eleanor Flexner
The Pursuit of Zero	The Lincoln Imp
The Lucky Charm	Jack Lait, Jr.
Two Poems	Beatrice Wadhams
To a Friend	James Flexner
Two New England Poets	Hope Hamilton
Book Reviews	Adèle Philips
	Henry Fox
A Page of New Poets	
I Stood Alone Upon the Rocks	Nathalie Swan
The Call of the Air	Gholson Kittredge
To a Young Poet	Lincoln Reis
The Path	Alwin Pappenheimer
I Wonder	Elizabeth Marshall
Folly	Anonybid
Coming Events	Dot
Athletics	John Van Pelt

| Editorials | First Half Dozen | Announcements |

VOLUME VI NUMBER IV

poetry has never been with us a classroom exercise but really
a by-product that had had no place in the regular school
program. Conferences, such as were had, were snatched
between "periods" or in breathless perambulations in halls
and on stairs. Our poetry, we always felt, was something
we did for its own sake, and that naturally we should use our
own time for it. (Here one might record a grateful word to
those teachers who endured, with never a word of complaint,
the interruptions to their classes caused by the belated
arrivals of these poets!) So of formal group instruction
there was none.

We early reached the point where a large group of boys
and girls naturally took over the question of values. When a
good poem arrived, endless small matters of technique were
the topic of general discussion. The poem is passed around
and fought over, but the teacher is only one of many voices,
each striving to be heard. In that hurried give-and-take,
bombast, posing, unclear or insincere thinking, are laid bare
in language more instructive than any adult could contrive.
The strong line that over-shadows the weak line, the brilliance at the beginning that makes a good end appear shabby,
the fine idea that is too good to lose in doggerel, the phrase
of astonishing beauty that is worth building up into an entirely different poem—these topics, I see, by my notes, are
frequent in the wordy and often noisy debates that greet a
worthy poem.

From these notes let me transcribe the incidents that
accompanied the final shaping of *First Snow*.[1] The editor
of the *Lore* came forward, having just broken loose from a
group who were chattering and gesticulating in a way I got
to understand; he was waving a manuscript. "Bea's got
something rather fine, I think," he said as he handed it to
me. I read it while he waited. "Astonishing!" I said.

---

[1]Page 170.

"Fancy a snow storm at night being likened to a violently egotistic clown!" I quoted exultantly:

> Pierrot
> Shows off to the stars
> To-night!

"Yes," he agreed, but with noticeable restraint. "That refrain is fine. Daring, too, to put it at the top and invite a fall-down later. But——"

"You wouldn't change it?" I wondered. This editor had an uncanny perception of values; I should not think of setting up my own judgment against his.

"Oh, no. It belongs there. She's strong enough to put it there. But—do you like all of it?"

I read it again, aware of the danger of those false first enthusiasms. "No," I said, "but I was so carried away by the picture as a whole that I didn't take in anything else. The last two lines——"

"Exactly!" he broke in. "Too full of thinking. Involved. The whole thing is light, light as the first snow, and she——"

"She stopped to think."

"Exactly! And Bea has no right to think. She's too fine for thinking; she is great when she's herself."

At that moment Bea interrupted with one of her flying entrances. "Jimmy likes it," she told me, laughing her most pleased laugh, but noting Jimmy's solemn face anxiously.

"All but the last two lines," Jimmy corrected.

We explained. She snatched the paper. "Oh, *how* I toiled over *that*!" She exclaimed with high disdain of her work. "The rest was easy, but *that*!" And she was off, with the crumpled script in her hand.

It came back smoother, lighter. Then we noticed that the next to the last line felt too long. Besides, a night had passed and the line had wilted. Some poems, we find, evaporate overnight, become less and less astonishing. So her next to the last line had suddenly put on a strut that was juvenile, elementary.

> Laughing to see
> That you are just snowflakes
> Falling on me.

In the halls, as she hurried to French, I waylaid her. "It's still too——" I began.

"I know," she cried gayly. "It's the next to the last line. I have spent *hours* over it but can't do *anything* with it."

We are racing toward the Frenchman's door where lateness is unpardonable. "And it's too long. Make it——"

"I have an idea!" she cried.

"Bring those pearls down to——"

"*Oh!* I've got *another* idea! All right! They'll come down." We are at the classroom door; she is backing in; the class is at attention and the teacher is under way. "It will come down"—stage whisper—"during the French!"

Through the glass door I wave a pantomimic apology to my good friend, the teacher. He grins back at me, shrugs, throws up his hands, points to both of us and taps his head. He understands.

And that is a partial and much-condensed account of the final stage in the making of one of the most delightful lyrics of this volume.

When the distinctive poem arrived we always made a ceremony of it at the opening of the next class. The occasions were rare, for we were careful not to give the honor to any but the best, and therefore we were able to put a right thrill into it. At those times, as I looked on the suddenly stilled and alert faces, I often thought of the boy Agathon receiving the prize for tragic poetry in the presence of those thirty thousand Hellenes.[1]

---

[1] A more pedagogical writer would surely add: See *Sympos.*, vol. III, *Dial. Plato*, tr. B. Jowett (Oxford).

"Before you begin your program for to-day," I would say, "I have something—rather good, I think—to read to you."

Fortunately for me their approval almost always seconded my own; but I err if I give any picture of dependent minds watching to jump to the windy side of the teacher's superior law. Those who know the Lincoln School pupils are quite aware that their training has not led them into that galley! No; if they agreed with me I felt surer of my ground; if they disagreed I questioned my own judgment. Their minds had been freed; they were, consequently, clearer than their more learned elders of all the petty prejudices of taste.

The news would spread quickly down the halls, sometimes overtaking the astonished young poet. Nothing was more encouraging to me at these times than to see with what generosity the pupils spent their praise; and to a new poet they gave sometimes a too-overwhelming tribute of honest admiration. In other words, they seemed to treat success in this sort of literary achievement as on the same level— well, almost on the same level!—as point winning in inter-class soccer. What more may a teacher of academic subjects hope for!

Sometimes, however, we began a period with a discussion of a poem that was so good in spots that one felt that something should be done about it. On one such day we accidently unearthed a word, new to that audience, *cliché*. An excellent poem of a sea-storm viewed from the shore had been spoiled, we thought, by the *clichés* of *tossing waves, forked lightning, crash of thunder* and the like, ending with stormtossed boats, smashed finally into, of course, *kindling*.

But the strange, and possibly comic, word *cliché* took all their attention. A lively-witted girl began to write rapidly, and with studied ostentation. In a moment she broke into the general talk with "Is *fluffy cloud* a *cliché?*" The laugh that followed answered her. She appeared dramatically dejected, gazing open-eyed at her paper as if she had just surprised a bug there. "But not *boundless blue?*" The laugh was even more tempestuous. "And *molten gold?* And *dewy earth?*" The class confirmed her worst fears, to speak pure *cliché.* "But surely," she brightened up, "*fettered soul* is——" Her sentence was lost in a shout. She shook her head, murmuring, "*Rosy sunset*, of course; and *hazy blue*; yes, I see," and dropped her manuscript with a delightful affectation of despair. "Someone is always taking the poetry out of life," she said.

Immediately she cheered up and began again with mock zeal to write; this time she was flying to catch up with the very wind of inspiration. Shortly I received the following illustration of the effectiveness of our teaching, a thing I treasure as a triumph of personal pedagogy:

B. C. (BEFORE *Cliché*)

Morning

I watched a fluffy cloud drift by
Across the boundless blue of sky
And saw the sun's rays, molten gold,
Upon the dewy earth unfold.

Evening

I felt my fettered soul uplift
Before the rosy sunset drift
And in the hazy blue afar
I saw the gleaming evening star.

A. D. (AFTER DISCOVERING—'EM)

Morning

I saw the sun with battered face
Trying to warm the human race;
I watched a sodden cloud limp by
Like some discouraged custard pie.

Evening

The sleepy sun in flannels red
Went yawning to its Western bed;
I saw one shivering small star
No brighter than our dishpans are.

For the sake of the art of teaching it is a pity that such intimate and natural material as I possess on the creative work of these pupils may not be publicly divulged. It were a profanation of friendship to do so. Nothing is given here but what has really happened in at least a small public way and therefore is general property. But the exhibition of the personal struggle to achieve is most fruitful in understanding this natural output of young life. In a way one senses the environment in which the creative spirit thrives, and catches a notion of the mysterious laws of its being; and sees, too, how simple and unlearned the whole process is.[1]

Generalizations and abstract principles, valuable as they are to right thinking in the field of education, are frequently of little profit to parents or grade teacher, who have not often the skill to translate them into terms of personal application. Let this be my excuse, therefore, to give a type of child reaction—I shall disguise some of the facts and purposely include data from more than one pupil, keeping the essential truth untouched—which carries with it its own warning.

A new girl had "handed in" a set of verses to a pupil committee of the junior high school, which were accepted as a matter of course and were mimeographed for general circulation in the junior high-school paper, the *Lorette*. Here they created no special comment until the editors of the *Lore*, the senior high-school magazine, pounced upon them with enthusiasm and printed them. That, perhaps, would not

[1] "If a child can write such a poem (*Gift*) at eight years old, what does it mean? That depends, I think, on how long the instructors of youth can be pursuaded to keep 'hands off'. . . . I think there is too much native sense of beauty and proportion here to be entirely killed even by the drying and freezing process which goes by the name of education."—Amy Lowell, in the Preface to *Poems by a Little Girl*, by Hilda Conkling (Stokes, 1920).

have concerned the young poet, as the thought of doing any-thing distinctive and unnatural could not then have oc-curred to her. However, the senior high-school students are not able to contain their excitement when a new poet swims into their ken, so must meet the young lady in hall and on stairs with sincere congratulations, the editor-in-chief of the *Lore* himself remembering to hold her on the way to classes with a fine speech of praise.

The next morning her mother was waiting for me, a woman of rare understanding and sympathy. She said, "I want to tell you about Clara, so that you will understand. She is terribly disturbed by the reaction of the school to her poems and says she will never 'hand in' another one as long as she is in that 'hateful school.' 'It may have been all right to print it, Mother,' the child had cried, 'but *why* did they talk to me about it, and before *everybody!*'

"She has been writing poems all her life," the mother went on, "but I have learned not to talk about them to her, although she knows I have saved all of them. When one is finished she drops it on my dressing table. After that she never cares about it but begins another. When she came to this school and found that all the children were 'handing them in,' she dropped her latest ones in with the others and went on about her work unconcerned, really, with the outcome. Well, the outcome was a shock. The praise that came to her from all sides frightened her, and therefore it angered her. I am sure she will get over it—I hope that no real harm has been done; we know so little about these things—but I came simply to tell you, so that you would understand what to do."

Clara's case illustrates something else besides the strange laws under which the sensitive creative spirit performs its work; it is one more example of the amount of verse that is written secretly, at least as far as the schoolroom may ever be aware of it. Our constant surprise at first was in noting the number of boys and girls who had been writing imaginative prose and verse but had concealed the fact. And even now, when the attitude of sympathetic interest makes "handing in" an easy matter, a group of inglorious poets, I have reason to believe, prefers to blush unseen. I may not tell how we found a complete volume of beautiful verse, too personal, and perhaps too amorous for publication in a high-school magazine—poems that had been compiled slowly for a year without a single hint of confession from the author. The editors of the *Lore* are invaluable here; they seek out and discover poets who would never bring their work to a teacher. Through a prowling editor I discovered recently one of the finer verses that we print in this collection; but incidentally I saw that the young man's notebook contained a score or more of poems which some day we may have—if we are not too indelicate in our approach. The effect of these illustrations cannot be understood unless one knows with what sympathetic understanding, from teaching staff and pupils alike, the work of the literary artist is received in this school. One wonders what terrible losses obtain in other types of education!

This sympathetic atmosphere visiting teachers note almost invariably and comment upon it. Pupils read poetry aloud without, seemingly, a thought of self-consciousness. The visitor, seeking a clue, wonders if a special literary group has not been selected for this School; but those of the staff who have seen the spirit of the School develop from the beginning, know that the achievement in spirit and in attitude has come slowly; that, like growth, it has put on its layers imperceptibly. Further, it is the result of a philosophy of education which, it seems to one observer, is common to the Director of the School and to the staff he has personally chosen to assist him, a philosophy which is not ready yet to set limits to a pupil's achievement at any stage of his growth, which believes that education is not put on like stucco on a wall, but comes primarily from within, which receives without question any sincere product, nor intrudes at every stage of growth with a too severe or too unnatural standard of perfection.

IV. How We Began

To THOSE who have wished more specific direction, particularly to those who have asked us how we set about to get such naïve expressions of the spirit as are illustrated in this volume, our invariable reply is to say, "Start with what you have and be patient."

In our first year of this experiment we had, until the end of the school year, only the child-like verses which with a deal of careful coaxing we brought to light from treasured notebooks and private hiding places. We found these in the eighth grade, the class that is now about to graduate. Others existed, no doubt, in every grade. Some of the earlier lines we printed and, with caution, talked about them.[1] Others came forth slowly, some fair, some very bad. All were received and made the basis of informal personal instruction; that is, we tried to show why in given cases the feeling of the poet did or did not become the feeling of the reader, an understandable criterion and one from which it was possible to begin. Sometimes the serious mood of the poet became comedy to the reader; often it was possible, without at all discouraging, to show why. Sometimes the verses did not make sense; at other times they struck up against insurmountable conventions, like the forbidden combination of rhymed and unrhymed stanzas; again we found unrhythmic prose posing as poetry, the discussion of which was always fruitful.

We never praised outright until we found the superior thing, be it an idea, a line, or a completed verse. But when that superior thing came—and it began to pop out here and

---

[1] Two of the poems found in these private notebooks, *The Afterglow* and *The Wind is a Shepherd*, are reproduced in Part I of the anthology of Lincoln School verse that follows.

there from most unexpected sources (unexpected to the author, I mean!)—then we cheered and spread the news afar. The staff as a whole joined in the exultation; and the Director of the School—instinctively aware of his part in the plot—was never too busy to learn the good news and to share in the rejoicing. Somehow we made the author feel that something really fine had happened in the lives of all of us: and, with the exception of the new girl, Clara, who was not quite prepared for our kind of joy in work well done, we do not know of anything but good that came out of this frank and sincere appreciation.

What we really look for is instinctive insight, something never imitative and never wholly from without. Professor Briggs, however, did approach it from without and achieved delightful results.[1] Rather, his study with a high-school class of the formal aspects of poetry awakened such interest as brought forth, unexpectedly, an outburst of creative effort which otherwise might ever have remained unexpressed. A volume of privately printed verse was the tangible result, *Lacrimæ Musarum*. But it is to be noted that the poetry came, not because of the study of prosody, but in spite of it. The main point in his experiment, we suspect, is that here a wise teacher permitted that overflow of spontaneous feeling and made the most of it for the literary end he had in mind.

And instinctive insight is too personal to be fashioned by someone else. Neither the subject matter nor the form of any poem in this collection has been set or even suggested by a teacher. That attitude of non-interference with the work of the artist is the basis of Professor Baker's success with his *Workshop 47*. "But Professor Baker never told one how his play should be written!" writes Perceval Reniers in "Behind the Scenes of 47 Workshop."[2] "That

[1] "The Teaching of Prosody: a Means and an End," by Thomas H. Briggs, *Bulletin, Illinois Association of Teachers of English*, vol. X, no. II

[2] New York *Times Magazine*, Dec. 7, 1924.

did seem to be a little tough when he was supposed to be the best teacher of playwriting in the country; seemed so, that is, until suddenly the student found he was doing it the right way himself. And this was a thing that the students who spared themselves in the matter of work, in self-analysis and in the bitter struggle of writing and rewriting, and rewriting again, never quite found out."

Poetry, an outward expression of instinctive insight, must be summoned from the vasty deep of our mysterious selves. Therefore, it cannot be taught; indeed, it cannot even be summoned; it may only be permitted.

And its practical use when permitted? Well, it is the hope of civilization. The only chance the world has, so many think in all parts of Europe and America to-day,[1] of breaking its old bad habits and forming new good ones is by fostering—not thwarting—the impulses of youth. The new education becomes simply, then, the wise guidance of enormously important native powers. For centuries we adults have demanded that youth shall fashion itself in our image; so the business of education in the past has been largely the persecuting of the unbeliever; and the beautiful religion of the child, which some of us believe to be the true faith, has been destroyed, its temples sacked. And yet we have never quite stamped it out; and we have never quite believed it evil; that is our hope for the future.

All this has been said over and over again by the philosophers. Let me give it again in the final words of one of the wisest of our modern thinkers on education:[2]

But with the dawn of the idea of progressive betterment and an interest in new uses of impulses, there has grown up some consciousness of the extent to which a future new society of changed purposes and duties may be created by a deliberate humane treatment of the impulses of youth. This is the meaning of education;

---

[1] See *The International Education Yearbook*, edited by I. L. Kandel (Macmillan, 1925).
[2] John Dewey, in *Human Nature and Conduct* (Holt, 1922), the chapters on Impulses.

for a truly humane education consists in an intelligent direction
of native activities in the light of the possibilities and necessities
of the social situation. . . . Among the native activities of
the young are some that work toward accommodation, assimila-
tion, reproduction, and others that work toward exploration, discovery and creation. But the weight of adult custom has been
thrown upon retaining and strengthening tendencies toward con-
formity, and against those which make for variation and indepen-
dence. The habits of the growing person are jealously kept within
the limits of adult customs. The delightful originality of the child
is tamed. . . . And yet the intimation never wholly deserts
us that there is in the unformed activities of childhood and youth
the possibilities of a better life for the community as well as for
individuals here and there. This dim sense is the ground of our
abiding idealization of childhood. For with all its extravagances
and uncertainties, its effusions and reticences, it remains a standing
proof of a life wherein growth is normal not an anomaly, activity
a delight not a task. . . . Our usual measure for the "good-
ness" of children is the amount of trouble they make for grown-ups,
which means of course the amount they deviate from adult habits
and expectations. Yet by way of expiation we envy children their
love of new experiences, their intentness in extracting the last
drop of significance from each situation, their vital seriousness in
things which to us are outworn.

However, we are not so gaily giving up our function as
teachers. Permitting those native impulses to play without
shame or fear of impertinence is in itself an art; and—here
is the point which we seemingly left stranded some time
back—our sincere approval when the inner spirit speaks its
true and individual note, that is the finest thing we teachers
may offer. For, we have found out, the poet does not always know, until he has been told many times, which is his
real self speaking and which is that other superimposed self,
the mimic and poseur, that crow with the peacock's feather.

If we are able, then, at the very first signs to approve the
right thing, growth begins in the individual; and, curiously,
others discover immediately what sets us elders agog, and, as
approval is very precious to them, and as they enjoy seeing

us agogging, the imitative personality is soon set aside and, for a rare moment, maybe, the shy, concealed self steps out.

Illustration may help others in this essential matter of judging the true from the false. The third grade had visited the docks and wharves and from a high building had seen the ships in the bay. When they came back they talked about it eagerly and then they wrote about it "so that others might know, too." The teacher, Miss Nell C. Curtis, guided them, of course, but without intruding. Out of the prose and verse of this reporting for others we printed in *Lincoln Lore* a column which we called *Songs of the River and Sea*.

Margery writes:

> I am the captain of a great big ship
> That sails on the open sea
> Rough and wild are the waves I love
> Come and sail with me.

Elizabeth followed with:

> I am the captain of a big ferry boat
> And I'm always, always, always, on the float
> And when the fog is coming on
> I blow my whistle loud and long.

These are commendable and sincere, but the following four lines by Peter are all that and more; they give us the picture in Peter's mind, and they did to us what all good poetry does: they made us, by means of mere words, see with the poet's very eyes:

THE WORKER

> I am a little boat
> That goes a-tug-a-tug-a-tug
> I pull the great big barges
> So slow . . . so slow . . . so slow.

Winthrop, however, did something else: he took us away from the scene altogether and let us into his imaginative self;

and because he gave us so unreservedly what flashed upon
the inward eye we found a complete answer in our own
imaginative experience:

A DREAM SHIP

Once a ship went by my window
It was a tiny sailboat
In a minute I was aboard
Sailing . . .
Sailing away!

He who has not sailed in this magic boat, who does not still
leap aboard as it goes by the window—well, "Let no such
man be trusted"!

Further illustration is needed, for the crux of the matter
is here: teachers, so I gather from many conferences with
interested individuals and with groups, do not always know
what is commonplace and what is the work of the artist.   To
teach one how to make that subtile distinction is not my
purpose here, although one must admit in all frankness that
without a sense for the difference the teacher becomes a
stumbling block to those who are groping for light; but so
much success has come from one type of illustration that I
shall take space for it.

Here are four stanzas written by children of about the
same age and on somewhat the same themes.   One pair is
what might be expected, imitative, ordinary, the other two
are the sure imaginative picture of the artist-poet.   Not to
confuse the reader I shall place the commonplace verse
first in each instance and follow it immediately with the
verse of the poet.

Last night
The rain came down
And all the flowers
Bended their heads

Sparkle up, little tired flower
Leaning on the grass;
Did you find the rain of night
Too heavy to hold?

In the same way I give first a stanza, good but not distinctive, followed by a poem wrought out of pure fantasy.

AFTER THE SHOWERS

The wind is blowing the flowers
   Sending out perfume of daisy and violet small;
But after the showers
Have rained on the flowers
   The smell is sweetest of all!

LILACS

After the lilacs come out
The air loves to flow about them
The way water in wood-streams
Flows and loves and wanders.
I think the wind has a sadness
Lifting other leaves, other sprays . . .
I think the wind is a little selfish
After lilacs come out.

Sparkle Up, Little Tired Flower and *Lilacs* were written by Hilda Conkling.[1] The other two are matter of fact; I am not sure if they are the results merely of seeing and thinking or of the sort of conventional attitude that comes from reading and being told. Hilda's verses, however, have that soft sure tread of the real person in a strange, lovely world, with no guide but herself, for none is needed; she colors her observings with a touch of her own philosophic self. In *Sparkle Up, Little Tired Flower* are pity and hope for all who suffer. ("But she may not know that—in words," as the

---

[1]The first in *Poems by a Little Girl* (Stokes, 1920) the second in *Shoes of the Wind* (Stokes, 1924).

eleventh grade told me this week, "although she may know it without knowing it, instinctively.") And Hilda's *Lilacs* is full of old myth. The wind is animate, personable, a little god, full of the prejudices and the jealousies of little gods. Hilda will always see the world that way, her way, because she is a poet. The other will see the world as she thinks someone wants it to be seen, or as she has read about it, until she takes the little step that leads her into herself.

V. The Non-Poet and the Half-Poem

Of course, the "superior thing" must really appeal to the pupils as superior. At first, I am sure, our own pupils did not know what it was that set a small group of us going so excitedly. At the very beginning, indeed, we have to admit a strong minority objection. At one time the question was debated heatedly in the halls as to whether the "magazine of literature" should not be abolished and for it substituted "something like the other school papers, with more athletic news and more good jokes." The teaching staff kept aloof, permitting that debate to rage until the minority were silenced, if not convinced. Later, as graduates, they have come over; especially as they learned to take a borrowed pride in the young poets of their alma mater whom they hear now and then spoken of outside with something of the faint voice of fame.

Our pupils, however, are not primarily interested in fame. Poetry is written for its own sake, because it must be written; and those who do not write poetry at all feel no compunction to work at it. I check off now a list of boys and girls who are interested in poetry to the extent of buying volumes with their own pocket money, of insisting that their birthday and Christmas gifts shall be poetry, who find their most comfortable occupation in unearthing poems for class reading, but who never consider themselves under any obligation to write. The appreciative and critical demands of their nature are amply satisfied; they know we expect nothing further from them.

On the other hand, I have in mind a group who write without ever once publishing, but who find their solace in thus expressing their moods and fancies, requiring nothing further. In personal discussion we treat these writers with the same receptive spirit that we should use with those of superior gifts. Just like the others, they write and revise, glow over the good line or the good thought, face the fact of this or that absurdity or crudity, all in the spirit of the mysterious creative art. And they understood our attitude thoroughly; they know that to us all sincere expressions of the inner spirit are serious and worthy; that even the most monstrous jumble might—who knows!—flash suddenly into pure design. Therefore we have no disappointed ones who try and fail and stop. There can be no true failure, so we teach, when one continually produces.

While some of these poets write with never a suggestion of change from us, many of them, even the most accomplished, bring forth astonishing malformations. Long ago, it seems, they got used to doing it, so accept the imperfection with understanding, often with the keenest enjoyment of its inadequacy. They are no longer afraid of being absurd! I have a folder full of copies of such half-poems, none of which we wholly despair of. Some are exquisite in parts, with hideous ends, middles, or beginnings. We laugh at them, and rejoice with unashamed vanity over the fine bits, and have faith that one of these days the whole will be deleted and amended, by a sudden command from within, into that perfection which—faith, again!—the Creative Spirit really intended all the time.

Here is such a fragment. I shall present only the good part of it. By the time this volume is ready for the press that fragment may have developed into the sonnet it was meant to be, but at present it is just an alluring octave with a commonplace sestet.   But such an octave!

BETWEEN THE WINGS

Between the wings some watch for spotlight moons
In whose pale flood they sing their madrigal;
Grotesquely solemn wait the old buffoons
To caper in the mimic carnival;
A warbling chorus makes its blithe advent
To tell of gardens painted on the props:
While I await the glittering descent
Of seven iridescent golden drops.

What that sestet shall be, only the author may tell.[1]   No suggestion will come from us.   To offer advice would be one sure way to lose it forever.   In five years I have not invited a pupil to write imaginatively on any theme suggested by me.[2]   To the question—now no longer heard—What shall I write about? there is never an answer.   There could be none. One writes imaginatively about imaginative experiences; no one else can decide in advance what they shall be.   So we drive them back upon themselves, drive them to search within, a boundless field and rich beyond expectation.   Perhaps that is the main reason for the individual character of Lincoln School writing.

Help toward finding that field, it should go without saying, is given in abundance.   "I can't tell you what you should write about," is the commonest approach to a new pupil, "because I don't know what you know; but I could tell you what I want to write about myself."   Then follows a vivid picturing of recent and remote experience, so personal that no one else would dream of using the material.   "That's

---

[1] That octave turned eventually into *Two Sonnets on the Theatre.*   See page 232.

[2] Which is directly opposed to the method employed so successfully in the French schools as delightfully depicted in *How the French Boy Learns to Write,* by Rollo Walter Brown (Harvard, 1915), and *My Class in Composition,* by Julien Bezard (Harvard, 1923), but whoever reads these remarkable books with any sense for values knows that the supremely important thing there is not the school program but the gifted artist who touched the very spirit of these French youths, the master teacher.

the sort of experience I am having, but, of course, you wouldn't know enough about that. Now you—what sort of experience have you been having? Where have you been? What have you done recently? What do you think about most of the time?" And so on.

Eventually—if one does not exact a "composition" every Monday morning—something emerges, and, like as not, it will be worth waiting for. We waited two months for *Nigger* and *Social Life in a Southwest Corral*,[1] two of the best pieces of transferred experience the school has published. The author, I recall, having some foolish belief that he could not write, begged for a subject, any subject; we refused, amicably, to be sure, to furnish a ready-made theme, but in the casual chat that followed, unearthed the Western year. Out of that came his only writing of the term. We have found few persons able to read those two stories unimpressed; yet they are plain unvarnished tales, even crudely written in spots, though you might not notice that as you read, for the total effect of dropping one imaginatively into the very life of an Arizona ranch is pure unpremeditated art.

Neither theme, then, nor method of treatment may come from the teacher! That will be the hardest lesson for teachers and parents to learn. But it is the only way if the aim is artistry. Painters know this when they teach. Theme and treatment are the business of the artist, never of the instructor. If that lesson is learned, if teacher and parent keep hands off and wait, personality will have a chance to express itself; the sign of success will be a refusal to receive help, as being both unnecessary and impertinent.[2]

VI. Self-Expression Throughout the School

THE poetic development of the high school has been set in a general school environment which is one of the factors that

[1] Both were republished in *Lincoln Verse, Story, and Essay.*

[2] "It is a very ticklish thing to endeavor in any way to direct so young a gift. It will find by instinct its own nourishment; that is my belief."—WILLIAM ROSE BENÉT in Foreword to Nathalia Crane's *The Janitor's Boy and Other Poems.*

may not be neglected in an attempt to understand the special product illustrated in this book. Naturally, the teaching staff has been interested in all forms of written and oral self-expression; and the method of sympathetic appreciation and instruction applies to all who write throughout the school. *Lincoln Lore* has invariably given up a part of its pages to the elementary school, where everyone seems to be a poet; and the output of the junior high school has been rich enough to fill monthly the many mimeographed pages of the *Lorette*. While the *Lore* has printed only what its editors deem to be the best work of the School, the *Lorette* has opened its pages theoretically to all who wish to write; the editors of the *Lorette*, however, regularly decline contributions that are not so good as they might be, and, as the amount of material is always greater than the available space, judgment is passed in favor of what the youthful editors consider the best. The *Lorette* grew out of a pressing necessity. It was not possible, without the charge of priggishness, to set up for the junior high school the same standards that satisfied the senior high school. Yet the younger pupils must have their own level of self-expression if there is to be any later growth. So the demand for a junior periodical came naturally enough and was willingly supplied.

Further, the upper school may look forward confidently to the coming of children who have had their elementary training in the Lincoln School; for the spirit of the elementary school is to permit the amplest self-realization. A beautiful native art flourishes from the first grade on: the speech of the children reflects it, as well as their poems and prose stories; and the walls are gay with their naïve canvases. Here as elsewhere there is commendable absence of a too dominant teacher leadership; or, rather, it is a seeming withdrawal of the teacher, the very best type of leadership, for it is never obtrusive or irrelevant or needlessly coercive.

After hearing Christina Rossetti, Ivria, of the first grade, writes:

> What is red?
> The sunset's red
> When we go to bed.

Michael, boylike, sees another color:

> What is black?
> The smoke is black
> From the chimney stack.

So on Valentine's Day, Nathalie writes feelingly, and in unheard-of language:

> With love and a start
> I will give you my heart.

Nathalie, when in the third grade, composes for several minutes with the most serious preoccupation, and, having finished, tosses the result aside and joins the others. Products do not interest these energizing spirits! But a watchful teacher gathers it up and it becomes a full-page decoration for the Christmas number of the *Lore*.

The fifth grade listens to the reading of a poem which tells of the spot most loved by William Butler Yeats:

> I will arise now, and go to Innisfree
>
> .   .   .   .   .
>
> I will arise and go now, for always night and day
> I hear the lake water lapping with low sounds by the shore
> While I stand on the roadway, or on the pavement gray;
> I hear it in the deep heart's core

Each child in the class had some spot which he loved more than any other and wrote about it.   Richard invents a name

LINCOLN LORE

VOL. V   DECEMBER, 1921   No. 2

 ne Christmas eve when Santa was very busy packing the toys in his sled, he saw five dolls that were not finished. One had no wig, and another doll had no arm, and others had no legs, and Santa was very discouraged. But he put on the arms and legs without any grumbling. Then a curious thing happened. A great light shone in the room, and Santa knelt down because he knew it was the Lord Jesus.

Written by Nathalie Swan when she was in the Third Grade.

that even his family had never heard of although the place itself is dear to them all:

THE BACK COUNTRY

Two tall trees beside the door
And the crickets' shrill chirping;
The great old-fashioned fireplace inside
And the playhouse down in the orchard;
The swimming pool with the cool water
And the long waving grass;
The old Back Country I will always love
Oh, how I wish I were there!

I had the good fortune to be present in the third grade one November morning while the teacher—again it is Miss Curtis—wrote rapidly on the blackboard the quietly inspired words that came from all parts of the room as the pupils thought of Thankfulness. What mysterious thing she did to put them in so glorious a mood I do not know, and I doubt if she herself could give a completely satisfying analysis. The effect was simply that of a silent amanuensis; they spoke their thankfulness, she wrote; but by some miracle of personal influence she had led them to speak out unafraid, and the result was poetry.

A footnote of warning must always be added; for one errs if deduction is drawn that our type of creative artistry is obtained simply by permitting children to be natural, to do as they please, to grow without cultivation or special nourishment like the lilies of the field. The secret of our results lies in the environment which we as teachers skilfully and knowingly set up day by day and hour by hour. Children do behave naturally, we trust, in the presence of the influences that the school consciously brings to bear; they are not aware, usually, that our direction is important, but we are aware of it at every moment.

The surface picture of children toiling mightily and with

huge interest at worthy tasks has led many an enthusiastic reporter astray. In presenting the material given above before the New York Society for the Experimental Study of Education[1] I fell unwittingly into the snare myself because in the short time that was allotted me I touched only the seeming naturalness of the creative effort without indicating the means which the teacher must continuously employ, particularly in the elementary grades, to keep the creative impulses moving toward right productive ends.

This free creating spirit in the elementary school is matched in the high school in classes other than English, as is so splendidly illustrated in one branch of study by Doctor Knowlton in his recent book, *Making History Graphic*.[2] The inventive ingenuity of these pupils is given unobstructed sway in every study, including mathematics; a gently satiric article by one of the high-school pupils was accepted for publication last year in a magazine devoted exclusively to the technical consideration of mathematics.[3] Even the modern languages welcome the brush of the artist, and the imaginative skill of the dramatist and the poet, which reference gives us just the excuse we were looking for to present the work of an eleventh-grade American girl when her fancy plays in an alien tongue:

QUAND JE SONGE À LA FRANCE
Par Beatrice Wadhams

Quand je songe à la France
  Un étrange sentiment
Me rend heureux—me charme.

. . . .

Petits enfants

---

[1]Reprinted as "English, an Expression of the Activities of Everyday Life," in the *Journal of Educational Method*, March, 1923.

[2]*Making History Graphic*, by Daniel C. Knowlton (Scribners, 1925), an account of the use of graph, cartoon, illustration, and dramatization in history by pupils of the high-school department of the Lincoln School.

[3]"The Pursuit of Zero," by Emma Rounds, *Mathematics Journal*, October, 1924.

Rose et gris,
Comme de petits phantômes
Dansent et rient—
Le rire de ceux
Qui bravent les larmes
Et dans leurs yeux
Toujours, toujours je vois
La vraie et belle confiance,
Qui vient de la foi
Et de l'espérance.

VII. The Classroom Environment

Visitors have found our high-school pupils preparing programs of literature for class presentation. At one time it might be Keats, Shelley, Wordsworth; at another time the sonnet sequences of Sidney and Shakespeare; more frequently the galaxy of modern British and American versifiers. It is then that they have asked eagerly for our course of study. Well, we have had the courage to have none. Who could tell in advance that a tenth grade would desire to equip themselves with the *Oxford Book of English Verse* and make it the basis of a half year's study? Or that an eleventh grade would agree to list the outstanding novels and plays for the past two hundred years, and to resolve, liking or not liking, to take their stand with educated persons the world over by knowing intimately the major representative productions of the past? As teachers we may rest serene, we think, if our classes are moving forward, especially if they have the powerful stimulus of self-initiation in the right direction.

At present the three upper high-school classes have settled themselves into something that looks on the surface like a fixed course of literary study. But it represents merely the needs and aspirations of those classes in this year of grace; time and the hour will doubtless give a different shaping to those courses as other classes come up.

The tenth grade are going through a standard text on the history of literature,[1] slipping along, stopping where necessary, using it not at all for study but for information and reference. Our main concern is with literature itself. As illustration for the earlier period we read *Puck of Pook's Hill*, the chapters "On the Great Wall" and "The Winged Hats"; and *Lancelot and Elaine* from the *Idylls of the King*. To get a better acquaintance with the famed Elizabethans we read from Noyes's *Tales of the Mermaid Tavern* (*A Coiner of Angels* and a part of *The Golden Hind*). In December they were lost in the delightful horror of *Macbeth*, but, with the sprightliness of youth, turned to the putting on of the Christmas play, *The Fourth Dementia*, a work of pure nonsense written especially for them by the teacher. But that will not prevent them from turning back to Shakespeare in January when *Twelfth Night* is to be read, and possibly played, in class. In the meantime they have been reading, both in and out of class, the Elizabethan section of Palgrave's *Golden Treasury*. This class may not be held here, as was the previous tenth grade, who gave the old songs in their original settings and made new airs for themselves and sang them right lustily.

The eleventh grade, following undoubtedly the lead of last year's rather brilliant class, are centering on modern verse. Committees have divided up the field and are reporting their finds daily. Their method is quite simple: to bring to class what in their judgment are the best poems of an author or of a group of authors and to read them to one another, with only so much comment as is needful or suggested by discussion. It is a spontaneous and natural exercise, quite un-school-like in its general appearance, and always enjoyable. Perhaps some of the effect is due to the fact that they have been permitted to form themselves into a literary society, the Robert Frost Club, and to carry on their programs with only such

[1]*English Literature*, by John L. Haney (Harcourt, 1920).

help from the teacher as he may contribute as a fellow member. No textbook as such is possible; they range through the complete works of the poets under review and everlastingly thumb the worn pages of Monroe and Henderson, Wilkinson, Untermeyer, Rittenhouse, Braithwaite, and Burton Stevenson.[1]

In a similar organization last year the class found it imperative to know the father of modern American poetry, Whitman; and it was not long before the whole group were refreshing their memories of Shelley, Keats, and even the Elizabethans. My notes tell me of the oft-expressed opinion that "the only way to appreciate the power and the beauty of *To a Nightingale, The West Wind, Adonais,* or *The Eve of Saint Agnes* is to have first a thorough acquaintanceship with the best contemporary verse" (which means, my guess is, that the best poetry is appreciated only after one has had experience with the best poetry!). The present class may drift in that direction naturally; and they may not. One indication is before me: a young girl who has been fascinated by *The Hound of Heaven* has asked if she might not present Shelley and Thompson together. "They belong together, you know," she said. "Yes, I do know," I thought, and marveled again at the unaccountable wisdom of these free young people. Her pure enthusiasm may start the whole pack "down the nights and down the days"; who knows?

The twelfth grade has taken the drama for special study. Poetry does come in abundantly, of course; Kreymborg's *When the Willow Nods* was recently done by one of them with exquisite care for the values of the spoken word, and, of course, they continue to write verse; but the aim at the outset was simply to acquaint themselves with the best drama,

---

[1]*The New Poetry,* Monroe and Henderson (Macmillan); *New Voices,* Wilkinson (Macmillan); *Modern American Poetry, Modern British Poetry, American Poetry Since 1900,* Untermeyer (Houghton Mifflin); *The Little Book of Modern Verse, The Second Book of Modern Verse,* Rittenhouse (Houghton Mifflin); *Anthology of Magazine Verse* (eleven volumes) Braithwaite (Small, Maynard); *Home Book of Verse,* Stevenson (Holt).

Continental, British, and American. Ibsen, Andreyev, Sudermann, Galsworthy, Pinero, Moody, Kreymborg, O'Neill have already been illustrated by selected dramatic readings. Dickinson, Quinn, Leonard, Cohen, Mantel, Matthews—collections all—are their main texts.[1] I am wondering if they will be in Euripides and Aristophanes before long. It may be; they went eagerly to Sir John Martin Harvey's production of *Œdipus Rex* last year, but they divided seriously on the value of the tragedy.[2]

For the sake of making doubly clear the sort of literary judgment which these pupils exhibit when left free to choose, and to indicate their level of literary enjoyment, let me give an early section of the programs presented by a combined eleventh and twelfth grade when studying contemporary poetry. This field is even more interesting to us because literary judgments have not been so inevitably set up for the pupils as would be the case in any older literature. Before that, however, one should note that in this school the interest in literature has followed rather than preceded the writing of literature. First there were poets and then literature appeared in the classroom a live and sincere thing. And, further, with all the extensive reading—some pupils now read anthologies straight through as other persons read books of prose—there seems no discernible imitative touch in the self-created verses. Each poet here has his own individual song. Imitation may be the sincerest flattery but

---

[1]*Chief Contemporary Dramatists*, First and Second Series, Dickinson (Houghton Mifflin); *Representative American Plays*, Quinn (Century); *Contemporary American Plays*, Quinn (Scribner); *The Atlantic Book of Modern Plays*, Leonard (Atlantic Monthly Press); *One-Act Plays*, Cohen (Houghton Mifflin); *The Best Plays of 1919–1920, 1920–1921, 1921–1922, 1922–1923, 1923–1924*, Mantel (Small, Maynard); *Chief European Dramatists*, Matthews (Houghton Mifflin).

[2]Writes a tenth-grade boy, "We left the theatre with a curious feeling of satisfaction, as if the play had quenched some dormant thirst. Probably not many will admit that they ever had a thirst (dormant or otherwise) for Greek tragedy, yet at the same time, I doubt if any will deny that there was a strangely pleasant reaction after it was over." A girl of the same grade writes, "King Œdipus was a man with whom Fate had played and then had tossed aside, ruined and broken. What had he done that, guiltless and unwitting, he should be sucked under such a whirlpool of disgrace, misfortune, and sorrow? He had lost all because of nothing—through a breath of chance. . . . Somehow, one failed to see a way in which anything could have been prevented. It was irrevocable; it was in the fall of the dice! The bitter irony of the thing cut one, like the lash of a whip, and one was left with a sense of smallness, of weakness, of hopelessness about life in general."

it is also the sign of the unoccupied mind; he who has learned to sing his own note has no need to borrow.

The programs represent a selection by committees of pupils of poems to be presented before the class in their literary meetings; the titles and sources were taken down by the class secretary and later placed upon the bulletin board for reference. I omit the names of committees and readers, and the notations on the type of discussion, biographical and critical; the point is simply to illustrate the kind of verse these pupils believe to be worthy, for the larger purpose of gathering here all the data needful for an understanding of the school setting out of which the accompanying selections of poetry have so naturally come.

The "volumes of verse" cited represent simply the books used as sources for the selections. The poets are given in the order in which they were presented among the programs of the class.

JOHN MASEFIELD

Volumes of Verse:
  Salt Water Ballads
  Dauber

Selections:
  Prayer
  Vagabond
  Seekers
  Laugh and Be Merry
  Captain Stratton's Fancy
  Consecration
  Sing a Song of Shipwreck
  Dauber

CARL SANDBURG

Volumes of Verse:
  Chicago Poems
  Smoke and Steel

Selections:
  The Fog
  Aprons of Silence
  Helga
  Night-Stuff
  The Crapshooters
  Wind-flower Leaf
  Up-stream

WILLIAM ROSE BENÉT

Volumes of Verse:
  Merchants from Cathay
  Moons of Grandeur
  The Great White Wall
  The Burglar of the Zodiac
  The Falconer of God

Selections:
  The Smooth Sliding Mincius
  Primum Mobile
  The Falconer of God
  The World's Desire
  People
  Merchants from Cathay

ALFRED NOYES

Volumes of Verse:
  Collected Poems (Two volumes)

Selections:
  The Barrel-Organ
  Forty Singing Seamen
  The Avenue of the Allies
  The Union
  Beyond Death
  Our Lady of the Twilight
  Ballad of the Easier Way
  Searchlights
  To a Pessimist

Edna St. Vincent Millay

Volumes of Verse:
Renascence
A Few Figs from Thistles
Second April

Selections:
Renascence
Eel Grass
The Penitent
The Unexplorer
God's World
Wet Rocks
Travel
Persephone
The First Fig
The Second Fig
Thursday

Amy Lowell

Volumes of Verse:
Pictures of the Floating World
Sword Blades and Poppies
A Dome of Many-Colored Glass

Selections:
The Fool Errant
The Road to Avignon
Mirage
The Pleiades
The Way
Suggested by a Cover of a Volume of Keats' Poems
Laqueries (4)
Ombre Chinoise
A Decade
Grotesque
Good Gracious!
Lilacs
The Madonna of the Evening Flowers
Patterns

ARTHUR GUITERMAN

Volumes of Verse:
  The Mirthful Lyre
  The Laughing Muse

Selections:
  Philosophers
  Survival of the Fittest
  Rules for Editorial Writing
  The Quest of the Ribband
  Strictly Germ-Proof
  The Passionate Suburbanite to His Love
  This Is She
  Logic
  Fiction
  June
  Mere Literature

JAMES OPPENHEIM

Volumes of Verse:
  Monday Morning and Other Poems
  Songs for a New Age
  The Book of Self
  The Solitary

Selections:
  The Excursion Boat (A part)
  Saturday Night (A part)
  The Slave
  Let Nothing Bind You
  Tasting Earth
  Jottings
    Arrival and Departure
    Listen
  I Could Write the Psalms Again
  The Runner of the Skies
  Self (Parts II, IX, XIII)
  Memories of Whitman and Lincoln
  Mist
  Rain Song

VACHEL LINDSAY

Volumes of Verse:
　Golden Whales of California
　The Congo and Other Poems
　The Chinese Nightingale

Selections:
　The Potatoes' Dance
　General William Booth Enters into Heaven
　Abraham Lincoln Walks at Midnight
　Niagara
　Yankee Doodle
　Alexander Campbell
　Daniel
　Apple Blossom Snow Blues
　Congo
　Litany of the Heroes
　The Chinese Nightingale

SIDNEY LANIER

Volume of Verse:
　Collected Poems

Selections:
　The Marshes of Glynn
　How Love Looked for Hell
　The Song of the Chattahoochee
　The Mocking Bird

THE DIAL POETS[1]

Selections:
　Sherwood Anderson
　　The Dumb Man
　　The Man with the Trumpet
　Dudley Poore
　　Marigold Pendulum

[1]So named, by the four boys who made the report, on the ground that these were the type of poets who are found mainly in the *Dial*. They were not particularly interested in Eliot or Kreymborg, although next year they had quite a go with Kreymborg; Anderson held their attention, but Poore's *Marigold Pendulum* fascinated. They read it many times and included it later in a program of favorites.

Alfred Kreymborg
    Adagio, A Duet,
    Dirge
T. S. Eliot
    Burbank with a Baedeker, Bleinstein with a Cigar
    La Figlia che Piange

MATTHEW ARNOLD[1]

Selections:
    The Buried Life
    Lines Written in Westminster Gardens
    A Summer Night
    Self-Dependence
    The Forsaken Mermaid
    Requiescat

WALT WHITMAN

Selections:
    To a Certain Civilian
    To Him Who Was Crucified
    Song of Myself
    As I Pondered in Silence
    To You
    The World Below the Brine

EDNA ST. VINCENT MILLAY

Volume of Verse:
    The Harp Weaver[2]

Selections:
    My Heart Being Hungry
    Feast
    Souvenir
    Departure
    A Visit to the Asylum

---

[1] No other explanation was given for the inclusion of the poems of Matthew Arnold in this list than the statement by the chairman of the committee, "He isn't exactly a modern poet, when you come to look when he was born, but we like him and think he will bear comparison with the others, and anyway, it will be a good thing to see if there is anything so different between an older poet and those writing to-day."

[2] New that season.

The Curse
Keen
The Pond
The Ballad of the Harp Weaver
I Know I Am but Summer to Your Heart
Oh, Oh, You Will Be Sorry for That Word!
I See So Clearly How My Similar Fears
How Healthily Their Feet Upon the Floor

RUDYARD KIPLING

Volume of Verse:
  The Truce of the Bear

Selections:
  The Story of Ung-Kay
  The Sea and the Hills
  The Truce of the Bear
  Amour de Voyage
  The Liner
  My Rival
  Road Song of the *Bandar-Log*
  L'Envoi
  Recessional

OLIVER HERFORD

Volumes of Verse:
  This Giddy World
  The Rubaiyat of a Persian Kitten
  The Laughing Muse
  The Mythological Zoo

Selections:
  The Friendly Cow
  The World at Large
  The Fauna of Australia
  The Chimpanzee
  The Early Worm
  The Mirror
  Nine Lives
  Catnip

The Prodigal Centipede
An American Anthology
Mrs. Seymore Fentolin
The Belated Violet
The Sphinx
The Salamander
The Mermaid
The Harpy
The Biotaur

ADELAIDE CRAPSEY

Volume of Verse:
  Verse (1915)

Selections:
  Cinquaines
    November Night
    Moon-Shadow
    Winter
    Night Winds
    The Warning
  Rapunzel
  The Vendor's Song
  The Fiddling Lad
  To the Dead in the Graveyard Underneath My Window
  To the Man Who Goes Seeking Immortality Bidding Him
    Look Nearer Home
  Perfume of Youth

JAMES ELROY FLECKER

Volumes of Verse:
  The Old Ships
  Hassan

Selections:
  Prologue from Hassan
  Epilogue from Hassan
  Riouperoux
  The War Song of the Saracens
  Stillness
  The Queen's Song
  The Old Ships

Ralph Hodgson

Selections:
   Eve
   Gloom
   Ghoul-Care
   The Bull
   The Bells of Heaven
   The Bird Catcher
   Reason Has Moons
   God Loves an Idle Rainbow as Much as Labouring Seas

Orrick Johns

Volume of Verse:
   Asphalt

Selections:
   Country Rhymes
      Little Things
      The Interpreter
   Second Avenue
   The Worker
   The Loom Girl
   Gold
   Song for the Little Mistress

Robert Frost

Volume of Verse:
   New Hampshire[1]

Selections:
   New Hampshire
   Nothing Gold Can Stay
   The Star-Splitter
   Dust of Snow

---

[1]Already familiar with the previous volumes of Frost they were eager to seize the latest volume when it came into the library and make a program of it. *Stopping by Woods on a Snowy Evening* became a favorite; *Good-bye and Keep Cold* was inveigled into a commencement address and turned delightfully to represent the parting of class and school. To catch the full sophistication of this spirited class one should picture our dismay and our fears at their parting from us and at the same time recall the final lines of the poem, "But something has to be left to God."

The Runaway
Fire and Ice
Boundless Moment
Stopping by Woods on a Snowy Evening
The Axe-Helve
To Earthward
The Valley's Singing Day
A Brook in the City
The Need of Being Versed in Country Things
The Two Witches
Good-bye and Keep Cold
The Kitchen Chimney.
For Once, Then, Something
Wild Grapes

Program of Favorites–So–Far

John Masefield	Sea Fever
Alfred Noyes	Our Lady of the Twilight
William Rose Benét	The World's Desire
Edna St. Vincent Millay	The Ballad of the Harp Weaver
	The Pond
	Your Face Is Like a Chamber
	Feast
	I Know I am But Summer to Your Heart
	Oh, Oh, You'll Be Sorry for That Word!
Adelaide Crapsey	The Vendor's Song
	The Fiddling Lad
	Rapunzel
	The Warning
Dudley Poore	Marigold Pendulum
Robert Frost	The Witch of Coös
	Stopping by Woods on a Snowy Evening
	Good-bye and Keep Cold
Amy Lowell	Madonna of the Evening Flowers
Edna St. Vincent Millay	Two Figs
Walter de la Mare	The Listeners
Vachel Lindsay	The Congo
Walter de la Mare	The Lamp-Lighter
Vachel Lindsay	General William Booth Enters into Heaven

Matthew Arnold	The Forsaken Mermaid
Ralph Hodgson	The Gypsy Girl
	Ghoul-Care
	Eve
Edna St. Vincent Millay	Recuerdo
	Portrait by a Neighbor
	The Unexplorer
Robert Frost	Birches
James Oppenheim	Let Nothing Bind You

The program of "Favorites-so-far" took three days to read, but they had no desire to shorten it. Some of the favorites named above had not been given in the regular programs but, discovered later, were passed around until they had won a place here. Others that might have been named here had already been used in a general program before the whole school a little while before. I have not included original poetry that came up naturally in these programs of contemporary verse; many of the poems printed in this volume had their first public reading in the literary setting of the major living poets.

These programs led us in all literary directions. Right at the beginning we stopped to know more about Masefield. Someone told about *The Widow in the Bye-Street*, with the result that it circulated continuously from hand to hand during the whole term. A word about *Nan* and we were off in a class reading of that bit of grisly horror *The Camden Wonder*. They found out then what literature could do to one! Much more of Sandburg was read, in whole or in part, than the program records; I have noted a long discussion that followed *Cool Tombs* (which they did not like) and *Chicago* (pleasing the unconventional immensely in defense of which they grew rather warm). The teacher, who could not always be denied, contributed with side excursions into his favorite Elizabethans, Romanticists, and Pre-Raphaelites, even managing to bring in Villon and Baudelaire. Poe as a modern imagist was one theme; the impish and provocative personality of Edna Millay—as judged solely by her self-revelation in poetry, of course—was another. One day the poetry was set aside while we dipped into *The Doctor's Dilemma*, but we did not stop until we had spent two days debating a far-reaching question of morals, Was Louis Dubedat worth saving? (In a straw vote the first day the Ayes had it overwhelmingly, but the final decision was a two-third vote of No.) A most fruitful hour was spent in recognizing the distinctive qualities in the blank verse as used by Shakespeare, Masefield, and Frost (My word for it, a genuine self-started interest and without even a tincture of literary pedagogy!) which led to the discovery of the varying texture of the sonnet as employed by Shakespeare, Wordsworth, Rossetti, and such moderns as Edna Millay and Rupert Brooke.

Visiting graduates—they always came to class with every college holiday—and visiting teachers were often invited to take part; sometimes they made their own selections, but more frequently the chairman of the committee would assign a reading. Books were handed here and there to likely readers. "Oh, let Liliane read that!" one would cry, and a half-dozen other knowing ones would exult, "Oh, yes! Let Liliane read *that!*" And Liliane, nothing loth, would take a moment to go through the selection silently, and then would read "that." And sometimes there would be a sudden general invitation for the teacher to read, a thing that never failed to send a thrill through him ("Flesh and blood! That's all I'm made of!"), and he would do his very best, as eager for approval as the next one.

Second readings are common, I note. They got to know that it takes more than one hearing to comprehend a good poem. The best compliment to a reader came to be the general cry, "Oh, read it again!" I note also that after a while a pupil might begin a difficult poem with the simple announcement, "I shall have to read this one twice." We discovered, too, that some poems are spoiled by a single extraneous word while others demand considerable explanation or setting in advance. Often we needed to tell first everything that was in the poem, so that our minds could then rest more comfortably upon the art of the poet. Technique in presenting the difficult printed word grew, you see, as we went along. Problems of enunciation became compelling; we found we were forced to sound the final letter with artificial distinctness, to "English" certain medial consonants (particularly *t*), to set off unusual words with pauses, and so on; and we learned to color the vowels, to use varying voice levels, to keep or suppress the swing of the rhythm, all depending upon the effect we wished to produce.

At the end of the term we had a Reading Party. Invitations were hurried forth. The room was decorated with flowers, there was an expressed desire to kill every suggestion of schoolroom, even to the point of hiding the blackboards with batiks!—and someone contributed a huge plate of nut fudge.[1] We read—and munched!—steadily for fifty minutes. Old favorites, among them *Marigold Pendulum*, *Stopping by Woods on a Snowy Evening*, *Good-bye and Keep Cold*, *Eve*, were given with that strange, rich effect which comes only with the rehearing of fine music; and a dozen original poems came forth as a special grace, *Beyond* and *The Clockmaker's Song*, for example; even the teacher, suppressing a native shyness in such matters, read out of his own private store a group that might have been called Poems Written in Very Early Youth.

The effect of these hours, everyone knows, cannot be put into words. The hundreds of distinguished visitors from all parts of the world who have sat with us from time to time as we shared these literary experiences, have paid tribute in many a vibrant phrase and, evidently, have spread some

---

[1]Could it have been the teacher? Taking literature from its stained-glass repository and subjecting it to the belittling association of "fudge"!

of the contagion of their pleasure to others; but those who have not been present with us will ever miss the first fine careless rapture. One effect reached the home almost immediately, which brought parents to see what was happening. "I came to tell you," whispered one mother who had beckoned me outside the door, "that my big boy is walking about the house reading aloud from Palgrave! My boy! Think of it! And he has been reading to me! Telling me about Wordsworth! Me! And out of my own book, too, the one I used in college and loved! And I let him tell me, and assume—oh, such an awful ignorance! What has happened to him so suddenly? He is so big. And his voice is changing. And he is so funny in his terrible earnestness. Oh! I want to laugh out loud. And daren't. And I am so pleased. To see this happen to him. Like that, you know!" She waved her hand airily. "And we thought he would never be interested in anything but gas engines. It really is too ridiculous! Oh, you don't know how funny he is and how proud I am! So I thought I would come up and tell you!"

It was not quite possible to sit unmoved among these mirthfully serious young people. One might judge the effect upon the so-called un-literary pupil—if such there be!—by the havoc played upon the feelings of the adults. Here is one auditor who is willing to admit that he learned about literature from them—more than he ever got out of any college class in the subject; many a time those hours have sent him eagerly off to the library and have kept him nervously up at nights scribbling away as if the Fiend himself had ordered a written assignment for the morrow!

VIII. LITERARY JUDGMENT

GOOD literary judgment is not different from other types of coming to a conclusion, in that it is based upon a fairly long and varied experience with the good and bad of the thing it presumes to judge. Experience alone is not sufficient, to be sure, but it is common sense to believe that opinion without knowledge is surely worthless.

Now the schools generally are built upon the notion— opposing common sense in this and in other matters—that judgment comes before knowledge. To be sure, it is the judgment of others mainly, not the pupil's own; for generations the classroom recitation has exacted answers from young persons concerning matters of which they could not possibly know enough to reply unassisted. To aid them the textbook was the storehouse for the opinions required, and the high scholar was he who knew the greatest number of textbook answers. "Who," the teacher of the schools might reasonably ask, "were the two most important writers of the New England Group?" As the book answer is "Longfellow and Whittier," no prudent child would venture to dispute. Although a good case could be made for Lowell, Emerson, or Hawthorne, a genuine exercise of literary judgment, under the usual classroom régime, would be disastrous to what the school has for centuries called "scholarship."

The college puts almost its whole emphasis upon knowing the opinions of others, the lecturer's opinions first, then the judgment of the critics. In college it is more important, for examination purposes, to know Horace Howard Furness than to know William Shakespeare. I recall a course in *English Poetry from the Death of Byron* that was too full of the study of opinions about the poets to permit time to read the poets themselves.

"What is the opinion of Pythagoras concerning wild-fowl?" asks Feste, the Fool, testing Malvolio's sanity.

"That the soul of our grandam might haply inhabit a bird," answers Malvolio from his dark dungeon.

And Feste, "What thinkest thou of his opinion?"

"I think nobly of the soul," cries honest Malvolio, "and no way approve his opinion."

"Fare thee well," says Feste sadly. "Remain thou still in darkness: thou shalt hold the opinion of Pythagoras ere I will allow of thy wits; and fear to kill a woodcock lest thou dispossess the soul of thy grandam. Fare thee well."

Although a Fool makes the test of Malvolio's wits, the above procedure has been the program of the recitation since Noah was a sailor; thou shalt hold the opinion of Blank ere the school allow of thy understanding.

Now the Lincoln School is not so much interested that its pupils should know what others think as it is to give its pupils continuous opportunity to grow in thinking. Expression of opinion, therefore, of point of view, of deliberated judgment, is one of the commonest of pupil activities, but it comes out of pupil experience mainly. Often this experience leads naturally to an extensive reading of the authorities, the conscious aim, in fact, of all the academic teaching; then we get something of the flavor of genuine scholarship as differentiated from "book-learning."

A single hour in the Lincoln School would show that here is freedom to think and abundant exercise in that freedom; that child expression is based upon child experience; that to answer "right" is to speak out of the fullness of living, not solely out of a book but out of life itself. One feels the freedom even from language self-consciousness; the thought follows a natural child form, clumsy and even comic from an adult standpoint, but adequate always for the end in view. Two fears are notoriously absent, the fear of not saying the right thing, and the fear of not speaking the correct set of words.

The main result is to uncheck the flow of expression; for if my answers depend solely upon my own experience I speak out freely and without fear, but if I am held wholly to thinking based upon another's experience, or to an alien and unfamiliar form of speech, I am robbed at the start of the very instruments of independent judgment. Now this attitude of the school toward self-expression is definitely connected with literary appreciation, as I hope to show.

My first experience with these independent thinkers came with an eighth-grade class. I had suggested the possible reading of *The Last of the Mohicans*, but was met with a voluble protest from those that had tried it and had found it wanting. "Everybody says 'Read *The Last of the Mohicans*,' and there's nothing worse!" was the dictum of one boy. However, I found a minority who insisted that the book was "wonderful and exciting." The debate that followed was a perfect example of self-expression gone slightly mad, largely self-righteous and recriminatory, each side accusing the other of a sad absence of good taste and literary judgment (I translate freely); but, I noted, it had a fine ring of honesty. Here was a time-honored literary dispute, clashing as only perfect opposites can.

To settle the matter we read the book in class, rapidly as one would read any story, with little comment as we went along. Although we made a slightly abridged version for the sake of time, we gave seven full class periods to the reading, for we were not only building up the material for an exercise in literary judgment, but we were possibly settling the question for these young people of Cooper, Scott, Dickens, Thackeray, and the literary dicta of their elders generally.

At times there was smiling superiority, or mild interest; at other times, outright laughter at melodrama whose trick of illusion had failed, or at the absurdly heroic and malapropos speeches of what Cooper called his "females"; but the long fight in the Island of Caves caught them as perfectly as writer ever desires to trap reader, and every word of Hawk-eye, the scout, was received with marks of sure approval.

I use the words of various spokesmen, which I noted at the time, to give a summary of their final unanimous conclusion: (1) "He didn't know anything about women." "Those girls are just sticks; you can't get up any sympathy for them."

(2) "The conversation is silly, except where Hawkeye talks." "Hawkeye is the only real character in the whole book." (3) "The Indians aren't real—just book Indians." (4) "But the fights are real." "Especially the battle on the Island." "That was perfect—you could see it." (5) "The fights with the Indians and Hawkeye—that makes it worth reading." "But without that it would be pretty wooden."

Is this good literary judgment on a writer so eminent as James Fenimore Cooper? Well, it agrees substantially with the conclusions of his greatest contemporary critic, James Russell Lowell, who writes—I read them the bit to stir their pride—in *A Fable for Critics*:

> Here's Cooper, who's written six volumes to show
> He's as good as a lord: well, let's grant that he's so;
> If a person prefer that description of praise,
> Why, a coronet's certainly cheaper than bays;
> But he need take no pains to convince us he's not
> (As his enemies say) the American Scott.
> Choose any twelve men, and let C. read aloud
> That one of his novels of which he's most proud,
> And I'll lay any bet that, without ever quitting
> Their box, they'd be all, to a man, for acquitting.
> He has drawn you one character, though, that is new,
> One wildflower he's plucked that is wet with the dew
> Of this fresh Western world, and, the thing not to mince,
> He has done naught but copy it ill ever since;
> His Indians, with proper respect be it said,
> Are just Natty Bumpo daubed over with red, . . .
> And his other men-figures are clothes upon sticks,
> The *dernier chemise* of a man in a fix,
> (As a captain besieged, when his garrison's small,
> Sets up caps upon poles to be seen o'er the wall)
> And the women he draws from one model don't vary,
> All sappy as maples and flat as prairie. . . .
>
> Don't suppose I would underrate Cooper's abilities,
> If I thought you'd do that, I'd feel very ill at ease;
> The men who have given *one* character life
> And objective existence, are not very rife,

You may number them all, both prose-writers and singers,
Without overrunning the bounds of your fingers,
And Natty won't go to oblivion quicker
Than Adams the parson or Primrose the vicar.

As literary programs organized by pupils are almost a daily part of our high-school English work, judgment as to literary worth is a constant requirement. Committees sit literally in judgment as they read, selecting and rejecting to secure representative work for class presentation. At these times no one seems to think of "looking up the authorities" or of seeking a teacher's opinion as a substitute for his own. Here is the thing of prime importance: they know that belief must come from conviction and not from authority. That is the essential mark of the training of the Lincoln School from its very first grade. And if one can conceive the paradox of an orderly obedient group living comfortably under authorities that they respect and follow, a group that at the same time is encouraged always to think freely and courageously for itself, then one has the true picture of opposing social forces harmonized by good sense.

If we are studying verse, then verse is the thing, not books on verse unless they are clearly indicated by the study; if we are studying plays, then the play is the thing. At the proper time the authorities come in, but always after experience has made the authorities understandable. Untermeyer's *American Poetry Since 1900*, and his prefaces generally, are quoted frequently in class discussion, but not finally and with awe, rather as corroborative of individual judgment or in outright disagreement. The pupils concur with him, I note, in his evaluation of Robert Frost as at the top of contemporary American poetry, but they believe that he has rated Edwin Arlington Robinson too high; and while they admit that Untermeyer may be right, because Robinson is perhaps too deep for them, yet they do not on that account go against the best light they have.

In a recreation period this year I dropped beside a boy who was deep in Huneker's *Iconoclasts*. I knew he was preparing a report to the class on *A Doll's House*—his own idea—and I was curious to see if he had needed to go to a book to find out what to think.

He read on for a few minutes and then closed the volume satisfied. "He missed it," he said.

"What did Huneker miss?" I asked, picking up the book and examining it, to preserve a casual air.

"That play falls down at the end," he spoke up warmly, "and he never sees it. Nora has three children. When she leaves them, the play 'goes out'—for me. It don't matter what she leaves them for; she had three children, and if she can walk right out of the house for good and not care what becomes of them, then I don't care what becomes of her. The play breaks up right there. And anybody'd feel that way. Now, Sudermann knew better than that. He wouldn't have done a thing like that."

"What would Sudermann have done?" I ask, but without appearing to probe.

"Take *Magda*, for instance. Magda comes home, a big success, after having been put out of the house when she was a child. Her father was the one that had put her out. Maybe he shouldn't have done it, but he thought he was doing right. Anyway, she comes back now, rich and a great opera singer, and the father wants her to stay. That's the fight—between Magda and the father. The father is a hard one, but, in a way, he loves her. And, in a way, she loves him. It's pretty even. You could decide either way up to the end. Well, she wobbles back and forth and then makes up her mind to go, and it kills the father. Your sympathies are for both of them.

"Well, you couldn't feel that way if it had been her mother; no matter how bad her mother had treated her. Sudermann knew that. It's the way we all feel. You can't help feeling that way or argue about it. So Sudermann gives her a stepmother. In *A Doll's House* Sudermann wouldn't have had them her own children, but Helmer's by another wife, or he'd have made them adopted children. Strindberg plans everything too, even to the old man's death—look at *The Father* (have you ever read that?) it fits like a glove— he plans everything out so that it seems all right when it happens. Ibsen didn't do that in *A Doll's House*, and this fellow"—pointing to the book—"what's his name?"

"Huneker. He has a considerable repute as a critic."

"He has, eh? Well, he missed one there."

The point is not necessarily to approve of the young man's findings, but to exhibit his relentless thinking on a matter of literary technique, to see him keep fearlessly along his own line and within his own limits of knowledge.

Again I must issue the caution that youth is not here permitted to express opinions merely. The world does that on every street corner, and if there is any gain in the process it is surely haphazard and fortuitous. The school differs from the world in that it presents even the material upon which opinion is expressed, it varies it to meet the growing needs of self-expression, takes advantage of its errors of fact and judgment—and of manner!—for educational purposes purely and gives it, finally, the kind of exercise that makes it a better and better instrument for self-improvement. And all this it does in the modern technique of the teacher's art, so imperceptibly—rarely by outright correction and reproof—as not to frighten off even the shyest of aspiring youth. Therefore we treat every opinion with respect, however ridiculous it may seem sometimes to us who are older and presumably wiser—with the same respect as a physician would consider a confessed symptom—and thereby we make it easy in our presence to speak out sincerely and disinterestedly. Outspoken sincerity we must have, for that is where the new education begins.

This is the explanation, in my best judgment, of the clear perception of literary values which visitors so often remark in the discussion and comment that go on daily in most of the classes of the high school. Professor Abbott reports one of his graduate students as saying, after an observation trip to the school, "I thought I knew considerable about Amy Lowell, but those pupils taught me something new in the sincerity of their approach and in the richness of feeling they extract from her poetry." Mr. Henry James Forman, after listening recently to a discussion, at times hilarious, of a fanciful scheme for rating authors ancient and modern, remarked, "They speak with such sure good sense; they have a standard that is both high and genuine; and yet they are not at all snobbishly literary. It is a marvelously healthy atmosphere for a young person to be in."

The explanation lies, then, in securing, first, a wide and varied experience with all kinds of literature, and, then, in permitting, without fear of rebuke, the freest expression of likes and dislikes. So I could rejoice recently when the eleventh grade broke into laughter over what they conceived to be the puerilities of certain late poems of Alfred Noyes. A storm of derision swept them; they read and broke down with laughter, affected exactly as we all were by the unintended comedy at the revival of the 1845 serious play *Fashion*.

The effect of these honest gustos was bewildering to one teacher-visitor. Her face remained grimly disapproving. "I should think," she told me in parting, "that they might have shown more respect to Mr. Noyes. Surely he is a better judge of poetry than any of us."

Well, is he? The eleventh grade felt that they had caught one of their favorite poets nodding and they had never been taught to conceal their thinking. "Would you have them show respect if they did not feel respect?" I asked her. She hesitated but answered firmly, "Yes, I would," but added, "certainly in the schoolroom."

Now, isn't that just what has been the matter with the schoolroom these many years! But let us examine the facts of the case in question, to see if we cannot make it exhibit once more the mode of approach that has given our pupils real power in literary discrimination, with its consequent effect upon their own literary expression.

Two committees had elected to report on Alfred Noyes, a poet they had been familiar with from the early years when they read *Drake*, and *Tales of the Mermaid Tavern*, and *Sherwood*. The first group had given us the well-known *Forty Singing Seamen*, *The Highwayman*, and several of the more serious short poems like *In the Cool of the Evening*. The second committee had distributed typed copies of its selections to readers previously chosen and was about to begin, when a strange thing happened.

One of the most able readers rose timidly and began to read in an inaudible voice, but she sat down after a line or two, obviously confused. It was a new experience for us; and as stage fright in the classroom is really unknown, I hastened to her, fearing illness. But all she said was, "I'm ashamed to read it—it is so bad."

"No worse than this one," came a calm, assuring voice from another reader. She waved her typed copy.

"It can't really be as bad as this," remarked another reader, exhibiting her paper.

Of course, we read the poems to see what there could be in them to bring out such adverse opinions where we had expected nothing of the sort. Well, their commonplace character was so patent as to be amusing. "Moon" was rhymed with "June" amid amazingly trite sentiment; there was a childlike discovery of "the heart of a rose," and other *clichés* that had already been laughed out of the young poets in that class. To see a veteran seriously falling into errors that they had discarded was, I suppose, the meat of their comedy.

I preserved one comment. A boy remarked, as we

gathered for a moment at the close of the period (to straighten out our faces!), "How could a man write stuff like that, a man who had done such fine things as *Forty Singing Seamen* and *The Coiner of Angels* and *Our Lady of the Twilight!*" How, indeed. That is the puzzle of the artist; but my own delight, I must confess, is that he did do them, for it gave me an excellent test of the literary taste of that group. Now I knew it could not be stampeded by a great name.

The next day I was able to bring partial confirmation of their right to question the literary judgment of their superior. Two critics whose authority is not easily disputed, John Erskine and William Rose Benét, had that very month censored the English poet for the same qualities that this class had discovered unassisted. Professor Erskine headed his critique "Arrested Development," while Mr. Benét in his title had asked ironically, "What Kind of a Noyes——?"[1]

Further confirmation comes from the kind of literature they really value. This same class has just completed a group anthology of modern poets, the result of a year's study in which approximately two thousand poems were reviewed in committees. Of this number about five hundred were considered worthy of a public reading. In the final judgment two hundred or more were discarded, while the remainder were sorted by the slow process of discussion and class voting into three classes: Class I, the best, fourteen poems; Class II, poems of superior merit, twenty-six in number; and Class III, good verse worthy of a place in a permanent collection.

The titles of the slender list of distinguished poems represented in their two upper groups are worthy of presenting here for the light they shed upon the literary environment which these young persons would set up for themselves—for there was a complete absence of teacher dictation—when left quite free to choose.

---

[1] "Arrested Development," by John Erskine, the New York *Herald Tribune Books*, Jan. 11, 1925. "What Kind of a Noyes—?" by William Rose Benét, *Saturday Review of Literature*, Jan. 24, 1925.

CLASS I: William Rose Benét, *The Falconer of God*, *The Horse Thief*; Adelaide Crapsey, *Triad*; Robert Frost, *Mending Wall*, *Stopping by Woods on a Snowy Evening*; Ralph Hodgson, *Eve*; Sidney Lanier, *The Marshes of Glynn*; Vachel Lindsay, *The Chinese Nightingale*; Amy Lowell, *Patterns*; Edna St. Vincent Millay, *The Ballad of the Harp-Weaver*; William Vaughn Moody, *Gloucester Moors*; Ezra Pound, *A Ballad for Gloom*; Dudley Poore, *Marigold Pendulum*; Francis Thompson, *The Hound of Heaven*.

CLASS II: William Rose Benét, *The Asylum*; Rupert Brooke, *The Dead*, *The Great Lover*, *The Soldier*; Nathalia Crane, *My Husbands*; Adelaide Crapsey, *The Warning*; H. D., *Oread*, *The Pool*; Walter de la Mare, *The Listeners*; Robert Frost, *Birches*, *Good-bye and Keep Cold*, *The Road Not Taken*, *Wild Grapes*; A. E. Housman, *From Far, from Eve and Morning*; Orrick Johns, *Wild Plum*; Alfred Kreymborg, *The Tree*; Vachel Lindsay, *The Congo*, *The Leaden-Eyed*; John Masefield, *Sea Fever*; Alfred Noyes, *The Highwayman*; Carl Sandburg, *Cool Tombs*, *Fish Crier*, *Fog*, *Grass*; Alan Seeger, *I Have a Rendezvous with Death*; R. L. Stevenson, *Requiem*.

CLASS III: Of the two hundred or more in Class III many poems had enthusiastic advocates for a higher rating, particularly these as listed with their authors: Richard Adlington, *The Poplar*; Rupert Brooke, *Grantchester*; Hilda Conkling, *Butterfly*, *Lilacs*; T. A. Daly, *Mia Carlotta*; Bliss Carman, *Vagabond Song*; Rose Fyleman, *Alms for Autumn*; Joyce Kilmer, *Trees*; John Masefield, *A Consecration*; Edgar Lee Masters, *Silence*, *Anne Rutledge*; Alice Meynell, *The Lady of the Lambs*; David Morton, *Symbol*; Alfred Noyes, *Forty Singing Seamen*; Edwin Arlington Robinson, *The Master*; Sara Teasdale, *Barter*.

The three poems that follow, *Stopping by Woods On a Snowy Evening*, by Robert Frost, *Eve*, by Ralph Hodgson, and *Marigold Pendulum*, by Dudley Poore, have received the tribute of many rereadings in the eleventh- and twelfth-grade classes. Found by the pupils themselves in their searches among the modern poets, they may be considered as illustrating one of the levels of unaffected literary enjoyment reached by the two upper classes of the high school.

Stopping by Woods on a Snowy Evening

ROBERT FROST

Whose woods these are I think I know.
His house is in the village though;
He will not see me stopping here
To watch his woods fill up with snow.

My little horse must think it queer
To stop without a farmhouse near
Between the woods and frozen lake
The darkest evening of the year.

He gives his harness bells a shake
To ask if there is some mistake.
The only other sound's the sweep
Of easy wind and downy flake.

The woods are lovely, dark and deep.
But I have promises to keep,
And miles to go before I sleep,
And miles to go before I sleep.

Eve

RALPH HODGSON

Eve, with her basket, was
Deep in the bells and grass,
Wading in bells and grass
Up to her knees.
Picking a dish of sweet
Berries and plums to eat,
Down in the bells and grass
Under the trees.

Mute as a mouse in a
Corner the cobra lay,
Curled round a bough of the
Cinnamon tall.   .   .   .
Now to get even and
Humble proud Heaven and
Now was the moment or
Never at all.

"Eva!"   Each syllable
Light as a flower fell,
"Eva!" he whispered the
Wondering maid,
Soft as a bubble sung
Out of a linnet's lung,
Soft and most silverly
"Eva!" he said.

Picture that orchard sprite;
Eve, with her body white,
Supple and smooth to her
Slim finger tips;
Wondering, listening,
Listening, wondering,
Eve with a berry
Halfway to her lips.

Oh, had our simple Eve
Seen through the make-believe!
Had she but known the
Pretender he was!
Out of the boughs he came,
Whispering still her name,
Tumbling in twenty rings
Into the grass.

Here was the strangest pair
In the world anywhere,
Eve in the bells and grass

Kneeling, and he
Telling his story low. . . .
Singing birds saw them go
Down the dark path to
The Blasphemous Tree.

Oh, what a clatter when
Titmouse and Jenny Wren
Saw him successful and
Taking his leave!
How the birds rated him!
How they all hated him!
How they all pitied
Poor motherless Eve!
Picture her crying
Outside in the lane,
Eve, with no dish of sweet
Berries and plums to eat,
Haunting the gate of the
Orchard in vain. . . .
Picture the lewd delight
Under the hill to-night—
"Eva!" the toast goes round,
"Eva!" again.

MARIGOLD PENDULUM

DUDLEY POORE

I

Dear, with this tawny marigold
I send you Ophir,

I send you Spain,
high galleons from Peru
wallowing slow in parrot green water,

I send you the gold house of Nero on the Aventine,
the throne of Babur, the bed of Semiramis,

I send you the dromedaries of Zenobia,
the beryl jaguars of Domitian,

the yellow desert beyond Baalbek,
fresh minted drachmae of Heliopolis,
rugs of Sultanabad, amber and green.

Love, look with favor on the gift
and the rest of my wealth shall be yours
by the next caravan.

II

Will no one deliver me from the haunted moon?
When I lie abed thinking chaste thoughts
she crosses the floor, slips under the sheet,
and cuddles her icy flank against mine.
If I move to another room she is there before me.
If I flee to the other side of the house
she looks at me from a neighbor's window,
or stands on a rain barrel to wink at me.
Now I am always listening for her step.
On dark nights I fancy her hiding in the garret.
In the cellar I look to find her flushed and tipsy,
sitting cross-legged on a claret cask.
She is faithful as an unloved wife.
Once when her scattered hair lay on my pillow
I threatened to kill her.   In derision
she drew a cloud over her breasts
and hid in the water jug on my washstand.
My thirsty knife severed only a long tress.
For a week now I have not seen her.
One of these summer nights I must find the way
to slip a knotted cord under her ears.

III

All night the wind ran round the house
hugging his sides with laughter.
Thunder tramped clumsily to and fro in the garret
dragging trunks and old bookcases over the ceiling.
The women folk pattered up stairs and down,
closing draughty doors, seeking each other's beds
to mix their long undone hair
and gibber like bats in cavernous twilight

when lightning thrust a yellow paw
in at the window.
I alone was glad of the tumult,
glad of the storm that kept me awake
to put my arm round the lightning's neck,
and clasping the tawny leopard against me,
to hear once more overhead,
through the hiss and crackle of rain
on the smouldering world,
the apple tree's gnarled hands
caressing the weathered shingles
on a night when I held
in the circle of two arms
all the sun's hoarded gold.

IV

Who tethered that white balloon
to the hilltop grainfield?
How it bellies and tugs,
whipping the guy ropes,
bending the oak tree pegs,
swelling rounder and higher,
crowding the very swallows out of Heaven.

Knee deep in the hayrick
the sun at rest on his pitchfork,
in overalls stitched from a double breadth
of blue sky denim,
watches the glistening bag of silk
that fills and fills
with mounting vapour of ripe meadows.

Oh, love, to climb with you
into the wicker basket of the wheatfield.
Oh, to loose the straining ropes of twisted sunlight
that tie the white cloud to the hillcrest,
and rise and sail
dazzlingly over houses and steeples,
to see red barns and zigzag fences,
pastures shouldering green elm parasols,
rumbling carts that yellow dust clouds lope behind,

dangling thirsty tongues,
chugging engines that pant
sweating up long hills in nodding bonnets
of curled ostrich or aigrette,
snaky rivers striped with bridges
writhing across the haze of level plains
till the sea sets an icy green heel
on their envenomed heads,
while swarming houses run to crowd the wharves
and dabble their toes in the surf,
where the sailing ships
clap shining hands on the horizon
and steamers toss dark windy hair.

Then at evening to rise yet higher,
rung after rung up the laddered atmosphere,
through emptiness like a hollow dish
to the highest shelf of thunder,
and there above cockcrow, above canon,
peeping over the world's tanned shoulder
down the pale abyss where the sun stables at night
to brighten his rusting harness,
and the stars polish their silver cups by day,
to loose a pigeon of lightning
from a hamper of storm.

v

On the barn's peak the moon sits washing her whiskers.
Now she blinks a green eye, slowly arches her back,
and walking along the gable on satin pads
glares at me hungrily.
All day she looked so demure.
When I lay on my back in the deep grass,
watching her prowl the sky eaves, and leap
over fences of blue
I never guessed she could show so thirsty a tooth.
To-night I am afraid of her.
I wish she had not seen me here at the window
observing her antics.
She is not nearly so attractive as by day,
sly creature, rusted with mange,

and one ear gone, I see, in the fight she had
with the orange leopard that owns the morning.

VI

Thunder hops on the garret roof,
rain scampers over the shingles,
old father God with a flash of his testy eye
slams the gold window of Paradise,
pulls a torn shade across eternal splendor.

On these rotted silks
where the moths' scissors slashed and snipped,
the years have wiped their yellow brushes.
Fold them away, dear, with the wasp-waisted spoons
in their flannel dressing gowns.
Let us wonder no more to whom they belonged.
It is enough to remember they will still be here
when we and our love are dust.
But let us sit with an open book on our knees
turning pages the pedantic worms have annotated
with crabbed wisdom and obscure geometry,
where mildew inscribes with a blue pencil
poems in forgotten alphabets,
and when the storm pauses
to shake the dank hair from his eyes
and resin the bow of his cracked fiddle,
we shall hear through the green humming of rain
as it lays a cold cheek on the cobwebbed glass,
all those curious noises that the dust makes
gently settling
on the cracked furniture of discarded lives.

VII

Summer's gold pendulum slowlier swinging
gleams through the fog-dimmed glass
of the year's tall clock.
Come with me, love, wrap your bright shoulders
warm in the swallow's cloak, and fly with me
over the brown stubble of reaped fields,
to rest side by side on a telephone wire

watching the loaded hay carts crawl important
like fat caterpillars down a leafblade of road,
or at evening to bend against the silver trance
of still pools where the sunset holds
long and long
the print of our wing tips,
till we find a lost blue key
that winds the intricate spring
behind a red pumpkin moon
and a nipped marigold sun.

VIII

They are all yours:
images plucked with the wild Turk's-cap lily
in deep reedy meadows guarded
by the darting regiment
of dragonflies in burnished cuirass.

Yours the songs I make
when weary with searching
I come with the tang of salt winds on my lips
and the beating of moth wings in my blood,
to hold my joy in the blue leaping world
and the tall dancing sun with yellow hair
against the wheel of my mind,
as the Greek cutter wrought
in the hard translucence
of sard or of jasper
the body of Eros.

Yours because all loveliness
is a polished shield in whose hollow
I see your eyes.

And my poems are a fire
lighted on the brink of night and death
where I hurl like driftwood
moon, stars, and sun,
kingdoms, galleons, caravans,
with hell and god and the four archangels,
the better to see your face.

IX. CREATIVE READING

THIS is a new term for a very old art, but the schoolroom knows little about it. As a rule, neither pupils nor teachers read well in the sense that I mean here; they do not transmit the message directly, as a good actor always does, making one forget the words, the delivery, the person speaking. There is a thing called the reader's tradition which so kills the possibility of a complete transfer and puts such a burden of interpretation upon the hearer that we all instinctively recoil when we see a speaker produce a manuscript. We talk so much better than we read; and when it comes to poetry, I safely claim that the inability to read, either aloud or silently, is the main cause for the failure of poetry to take its rightful high place in the lives of children. The high-school pupils of the Lincoln School have been brought to read poetry; our procedure there is one of the conditions that one must take into account in comprehending the literary environment of that part of the school.

At the outset we give our senior high-school pupils the experience of hearing literature read in the way we believe it should be done. During the first quarter of the tenth grade we hardly permit them to read aloud at all. But they are subjected to as many literary experiences as it is in our power to give

> of ballad, songs, and snatches
> And dreamy lullaby.
> Our catalogue is long
> Through every passion ranging
> And to their numerous changes
> We tune our supple song!

Ability to do this sort of thing, we conceive, is part of our business as teachers of literature. Something of the actor is in the requirement, a sense of feeling the part which finally "gets across the foots." Indeed, as I analyze the kind of

performance which has undoubtedly brought those young
auditors into quick rapport and has set them prying into
books of verse to secure for themselves the hitherto un-
guessed pleasure, I find that a sincere feeling for the mood of
the poem is the one indispensable item. Obviously it is not
to be had via "small beer parsing."[1]

Consider, for a moment or two, the different qualities in
the following pieces of literature and ask if it is possible to
give them their rightful values by an identical interpretation,
the usual type of reading, that monotonous sing-song exacti-
tude of word following word,

First, take Orrick John's *Wild Plum:*

> They are unholy who are born
> To love wild plum at night,
> Who once have passed it on a road
> Glimmering and white.
>
> It is as though the darkness had
> Speech of silver words,
> Or as though clouds of stars
> Perched like ghostly birds.
>
> They are unpitied from their birth
> And homeless in men's sight,
> Who love, better than the earth,
> Wild plum at night.

Recall now the dozen lines immediately following Macbeth's staggering entry, with the deed done and the blood
dripping from his hands:

LADY MACBETH: . . . My husband!
MACBETH: I have done the deed.—Didst thou not hear a noise?
LADY MACBETH: I heard the owl scream and the crickets cry.
Did not you speak?
MACBETH: When?

---

[1]Christopher Morley's phrase in a stirring, indignant, and vastly amusing article, *A Mirror for Magistrates*, in the *Saturday Review of Literature* for January 17, 1925, wherein he has the joyful ejaculation, "How shall we justify the ways—not of God to man, but of teachers to literature?"

LADY MACBETH: Now!
MACBETH: As I descended?
LADY MACBETH: Ay!
MACBETH: Hark!—
Who lies in the second chamber?
LADY MACBETH: Donalbain.
MACBETH (*looking at his hands*): This is a sorry sight.

Turn from that horror to the contrast between the lover and the mother in Meredith's *Love in the Valley:*

(*The lover is saying*)

Shy as the squirrel and wayward as the swallow
     Swift as the swallow along the river's light
Circleting the surface to meet his mirrored winglets,
     Fleeter she seems in her stay than in her flight;
Shy as the squirrel that leaps among the pine tops,
     Wayward as the swallow overhead at set of sun,
She whom I love is hard to catch and conquer,
     Hard, but O the glory of the winning were she won!

(*While the mother is thinking*)

When her mother tends her before the laughing mirror,
     Tying up her laces, looping up her hair,
Often she thinks, were this wild thing wedded
     More love should I have and much less care!

Read, finally, the tense fluttering and vanishing of human life in Adelaide Crapsey's *The Warning*, remembering that she wrote it at Saranac while waiting for her own near summons:

Just now
Out of the strange
Still dusk .   .   . as strange, as still . , .
A white moth flew. Why am I grown
So cold?

A true perception of literature—taste, if you will—is a knowledge of differences, of textures, of values, levels. The feeling for these qualities enters the very spirit of the reader and comes out in his reading; he conveys, by bearing, tone, pause, speed, emphasis, suggestion—whatever is intuitive in his personal equipment—just those distinctions which he knows to be there. Without this sure sense no reading is adequate.

Now, one might reasonably ask, how does one acquire this power of literary discrimination? Unfortunately, no one knows. Obviously it cannot be taught in the usual method of the schools, which comprehends always an analysis, a sorting out of elements; like all arts it defies the open sesame of the professional pedagogue.[1] But it may be taught by observation and by imitation. If the teacher is able to play on the four strings of his instrument, the music will be first appreciated and later performed. That is the conclusion based upon many years of observation of predictable results.

So for a large part of the term of the senior high school our pupils listen to literature. Having heard the interpretation in a given instance the listener can immediately play the air himself with the score before him, and can summon, as often as he pleases, the delight that he first experienced.

Not that at once he will read effectively aloud; he may not at first be able at all to read to "the sensual ear" but he may "pipe to the spirit ditties of no tone."

And at the beginning of each term, taking advantage of the time which committees of the class will need to formulate a literary program, the teacher reads, reads, reads. In holding their attention he should be expert enough to vary the spell, to surprise continuously with the infinite variety of his material. And even when the pupils begin their own programs he should frequently add to their selections, or take the page from them to show other possible interpretations. And he should never commit the absurdity of believing,

---

[1] "It were as wise to cast a violet into a crucible that you might discover the formal principle of its color and odor."—Shelley, in *A Defence of Poetry*.

following the most popular of our modern theories of education, that so long as the child is performing, no higher result may be wished for. Child activity is marvelously educative, in its proper place; but it is not a substitute for teacher activity, in its proper place.

In the reading, we never forget that the reading is the thing. Information is important only to increase the value of the reading. A poem read is something performed for the sake of an effect upon the auditor. The point is never, What have you learned? but What has it done to you? Literature differs in this respect from commonplace writing; it has the power to play upon the image-making self, to put pictures there, to stir unexpected emotions, to compel that lending of one's mind to another, which, at its best, is an exquisite release. To be able to extract from literature this its finest flavor is the gift of the creative reader, without which literature is not different from any other combination of words; indeed, without that gift on the part of the reader, literature becomes a thing obscure if not repellent. The commonest accusation against the literature of the schools is that it kills; I trust I have made clear one ground of that indictment.

The gravest defect that I have noticed in the reading of teachers is what I might call the evidence of too much respect for literature. It is all done in the same solemn style

> of uttering platitudes
> In stained-glass attitudes.

Literature is frequently grave, but is often jolly and satiric and sly, often purposely bombastic, uproarious, bitter, and even coarse, *vide* the drunken scenes in *Twelfth Night*. In a seminar in Shakespeare I recall now the writhings of a famous professor of literature while a high-school teacher, a student in the course, read Polonius's crafty advice to Laertes. She **read** it eloquently, with a tremble in her voice, as if it were the Psalms of David and not the windy platitudes of a commonplace bore. When the lady had finished in a lordly climax, the professor unwrithed and with a bow remarked, "All that I can say, Miss X, is that you have read that speech—too well." And the lady beamed and blushed; and all the other ladies murmured approval; and at the close they gathered around to congratulate her! Immediately after the hour I saw the Professor alone; he was pacing his small office nervously. "I thought at first," I said, "that you were too hard on her, but she missed it completely." He was grim. "They all missed it," he said; and added, "For less than that the Lord brought low the Cities of the Plain!"

We teachers of the æsthetic side of education need the common-sense attitude of the village milkmaid, Patience. She listens, you remember, at first obviously perplexed, when, all the ladies having begged so beautifully, Bunthorne reluctantly agrees to read his latest poem. But he warns them. "It is a wild, weird, and fleshly thing," he says, "Yet very tender, very yearning, very—precious. It is called 'Oh, Hollow! Hollow! Hollow!'"

Patience brightens up. "Is it a hunting song?" she asks, albeit timidly, for Bunthorne's manner is menacingly heavy, and she is surrounded by rich, beautiful ladies of the nobility.

"A hunting song!" exclaims Bunthorne, a little dropped, however, from his elevated attitude. "No, it is *not* a hunting song! It is the wail of the poet's heart on discovering that everything is commonplace. To understand it, cling passionately to one another and think of faint lilies."

The ladies all cling, except Patience, who sensibly moves nearer the exit.

And when he has recited of

> the writhing maid, lithe-limbed
> Quivering on amaranthine asphodel

the Lady Angela exclaims, "How purely fragrant!" And the Lady Saphir, "How earnestly precious!" But the simple Patience says, "Well, it seems to me to be nonsense!" Then the Lady Saphir, somewhat taken aback, recovers and restores the high altitudes, "Nonsense, yes, probably," she considers, "but, oh, what *precious* nonsense!"

As a beginning assignment to a course for teachers and parents (and governesses) in the reading of literature I should prescribe a careful study of every line of the libretto of *Patience* to cure them of ranking

> as apostles in the high æsthetic band
> Who would walk down Piccadilly with a poppy (or a lily) in their
>   mediæval hand.

A failure to see the humor and the sound sense in this satire of our profession would eliminate the student automatically from the course.

I trust the references to *Patience* will not seem a digression. It is most important for those who desire to understand how we have obtained certain results in the creating of literature itself to know that we believe the ability to read literature is so important that we have refused to take it invariably as a solemn duty ("I had no idea," exclaims Patience, "that love was a *duty*. No wonder they all look so unhappy!") We have set enjoyment as our test, and not duty. And we have sought to make our reading give us all the enjoyment that rightfully belongs to us. "Poetry is the record of the happiest moments of the happiest and best minds," says the wise Shelley in his *Defence of Poetry;* therefore we have refused to chant it to an unvarying *Miserere.*

We have had no "lessons" in learning to read. There has been no attempt at any time to formalize our literature in that respect. We read. But, as visiting teachers have frequently pointed out, we put all our attention on what the poet has to say. "It is as if they were reading a letter to the class," one remarked, "from someone whom they all know very well, and like, and really want to hear from; and all their mind is on what the writer has to say to them." Exactly. A poet has something to say, or he is no poet. And his way of saying it—vastly important always—"the eloquence of beauty," "the mild and healing sympathy," "the voice of gladness," these steal into our musings ere we are aware.

Let me select again from my notes on cases. The eleventh grade is exploring modern poetry. Two boys have just reported to the class their "finds" in the work of Joyce Kilmer. One has read *Trees* clearly and acceptably enough; that is, none missed its obvious intention. When they had finished, a girl spoke a brief word concerning a group of Sara Teasdale's poems that a committee had selected, mainly from *Flame and Shadow*. (The program of poems had already been placed upon the blackboard.) At her direction one or two pupils read; effectively enough; at least, one heard every word and had time to hear, the readers knowing now that poetry is difficult to listen to and that the hearer deserves every help of "Silence and slow Time." Then the chairman arose to read *The Crystal Gazer*. She was a good reader always, accurate, clear, thoughtful; she did everything with marked intelligence; but this time she was unwittingly to perform a little miracle.

Something expectant in her quiet bearing, in her eyes—they had grown strangely luminous—in the slow movement of her hand as she gently turned a page, something held us before she had begun. In consequence her first line was given in the most perfect of all silences, that silence within a silence, when not only is every bodily movement of the audience stilled but their minds seem to stop all conflicting vibrations and willingly surrender to attention. She read:

The Crystal Gazer

I shall gather myself into myself again
   I shall take my scattered selves and make them one,
I shall fuse them into a polished crystal ball
   Where I can see the moon and the flashing sun.

I shall sit like a sibyl, hour after hour intent,
   Watching the future come and the present go—
And the little shifting pictures of people rushing
   In tiny self-importance to and fro.

Eight lines and it was all over. We settled back, some-what startled at what had been done to us.

The reading that followed was all keyed high, a contagion was in the air, although no comment had been made; but when the period closed there was a rush to the astonished young lady and a shower of congratulations from teacher, pupils, and visitors, unique in the experience of that class.

Mr. William Inglis was present and will bear testimony to the things that were done to him by that reader. It amuses me to think that this one-time member of the editorial board of *Harper's* strode up to the girl and, waving a finger at her in an eloquent gesture of approval, talked excitedly, "I saw Booth do that once! Just what you did! Before he spoke a word he had a mob of indifferent people in a spell. He did things to them that night—to me—to everybody—as you did just now. And a marvelous thing you did! Marvelous!"

That was eleven o'clock in the morning. He had stopped by for another purpose entirely, but five o'clock found the editor still in the school and still vibrating from the marvelous thing that had been done to him!

The reader had felt deeply; she made us feel too. She was not aware of having scored so exceptionally, until we told

her, although she admitted that at the time she had noted
the sudden silence, a fall of silence, as it were; and she was
conscious all through of, somehow, doing better than she had
expected.   It was strong feeling projected, and my belief is
that she did it both with her mind and with her body.   That
poem was all through her when she stood quietly before us
and held us with her bright, steady eyes.   Stark Young has
many good things to say on this side of the actor's art—oh,
it is acting; all good reading is that!—and the reader of *The
Crystal Gazer* illustrates his point of view pat.[1]

Of course, one experience like that and a whole class is
taught forever.   They will all read better and better from
that moment on.   Fortunately good things spread; and there
is no teaching equal to feeling.

My next case is out of the earliest year of this experiment,
and it represents the first really great reading from our pupils.
We had been working in Wordsworth, Keats, Shelley; each
had selected a poem to present later in class.   We had no
other object then, I fancy, beyond the idea of familiarizing
ourselves with poetry that everyone save ourselves seemed
to know.   It was a small senior class, and college entrance
examinations—the first for this school—were impending.   I
doubt if any one in the class had a serious thought of liking
these poems; it was a thing to be done, and this was a type of
class that always did the necessary proper thing.   (I take
my motivation as I find it, making the most of what is already there.)

We set a date far ahead to come together and read, and
went on with other matters.   When the day came around I
recall that Miss Mildred C. Thompson, now Dean, and a
group of the faculty of Vassar College came into the room
and sat with us through the hour.   My mind, however, was

---

[1]In *The Flower in Drama*, the chapter on Duse.   In Note VI of *A Story Teller's Story* Sherwood Anderson writes, "Mr. Stark Young had talked to me one day of what thinking might
be, and his words kept ringing in my ears.   Such words as he had said to me always excited
like music or painting. . . .   He had said that thinking meant nothing at all unless it was
done with the whole body—not merely with the head."

on a young girl who entered with the others. It was her first return after the death of one very near to her, the dearest of chums and the best playfellow she would ever know. She had said to us the day before, "I am not afraid to come back now. I am all right now—if they will not talk to me about it. I couldn't stand it if they talked to me about it. I would break; and I know—I know he . . . would not want me to do that."

We read. I remember hiding my concern by excessive gayety over my own interpretation of *The Grecian Urn* (I am one of those who think it has a passage of the rarest crystal humor, but few teachers have been able to find it unassisted); but all the while I was thinking that before she had gone so suddenly out of class, she had selected for her study and reading the *Ode to the Nightingale* whose theme is Death. And she was smiling brightly at my fooling, with her Keats open before her. I took advantage of a diversion to say quietly to her, "You need not read, you know."

"Oh," she understood, "I want to read. Don't be afraid. It is all right. I have been reading it ever since. It has consoled me as nothing else could."

I tried to delay the program, hoping for the closing bell, but only succeeded in giving her the position of climax at the end of the hour.

In the first dozen words everyone, including our guests, were aware of a strange sincerity in the reading:

> My heart aches, and a drowsy numbness pains
>   My sense, as though of hemlock I had drunk
> Or emptied some dull opiate to the drains
>   One minute past, and Lethe-wards had sunk.

Such reading! And such trembling attention! With a passion that those fine lines have held ready for a hundred years and more, she went on

Darkling I listen; and for many a time
I have been half in love with easeful Death. . . .
Now more than ever seems it rich to die,
  To cease upon the midnight with no pain
  While thou art pouring forth thy soul abroad
      In such ecstasy!

For us the last few lines were terrible with personal meaning

  Adieu! Adieu! Thy plaintive anthem fades
  Past the near meadows, over the still streams,
  Up the hill-side; and now 'tis buried deep
    In the next valley-glades:
  Was it a vision, or a waking dream!
  Fled is that music.—Do I wake or sleep?

Other illustrations crowd, but one cannot paint a cry, as old Hieronimo long ago insisted, or word the brave anguish of bereavement. I think now of a boy quietly reading a scene from Andreyev's *Anathema*, where the devil, having first tempted old David Leizer to take a fortune, now tempts him to give it all to the needy. The poor, the lame, and the sick crowd upon him as he gives; they grow in number, the poor, the lame, and the sick, the maimed children—pitiful!—and the mothers of the children. And then come the blind, crowding, crowding, and David Leizer has no more to give; they crowd him, the blind, and feel tremblingly his body and seek to know his dear features with their hands, while they continue to cry, "So this is David Leizer! This is David Leizer, who will care for us now! David! David! David Leizer!" And the curtain falls slowly with the exulting cry of the blind. But David, his fortune given away, is weeping painfully, for who can bind up the wounds of the world!

The reading was expressionless, monotonous; but that boy put that scene into our minds so that it is likely to stay with us. He made us feel it for the remainder of our days; because he felt it himself.

X. Unsupervised Reading

Outside reading has been almost entirely voluntary, but it has been done well; and it has counted enormously in giving us a setting for our creative work. How this unsupervised "reading for pleasure" has been kept at its commendable level is another story; the point in this analysis is to note that, both in the type of book read and in the "spread" of good reading among the pupils, the results have been increasingly desirable: almost everyone now reads nonfiction easily; the standard of pleasure-in-reading for all classifications (fiction, verse, drama, essay) is high; the "return," in chat and discussion and in brief book report and long article, is all that we might ask for. Best of all, the spirit of the comment on reading is natural and truthful; therefore it is often felicitously put[1] and—therefore, again!— often strangely wise. No school-book "categories" are even remotely referred to, for these young persons know little about such matters; but daily the strongest kind of distinction is drawn by those young readers, in values, in relationships, in form and design, in measures of feeling, in sense of phrasing, in mass effect and the like, with never the need of any specially learned vocabulary.

The importance of securing a receptive audience must be stressed. Your occasional poet may always be found, and the teacher with a flair for that sort of thing himself may do much to stimulate imaginative power; but nothing in all the teacher's art can equal in potency the effect of the pupil's own contemporaries. If they are ignorant of literary

---

[1] As in this book report by a tenth-grade boy: When a book is as widely read and as highly praised as *David Copperfield*, it seems almost heresy to make an unfavorable comment, yet I did not like it. The story seemed to me long-winded and uninteresting, and a large number of the incidents of which it is composed unbearably sentimental. The characters appeared greatly overdrawn, all the way from Agnes, the tender innocent, to Mr. Micawber, the humorous ne'er-do-well. I never would have finished *David Copperfield* if I had not felt that it was a necessary part of my education.

experience—that ciliated uprising of Benét or the cervical thrill of Phelps—they have an unholy power to blight; if, however, they have been genuinely stirred by literature, if good reading is really a part of their life, they will behave toward poets as would any other intelligent and cultured audience—better, indeed, for adults in the mass have a deft habit of pretending to good taste by following the lead of the hour, and, for the same reason, maturer persons are less free to stress their honest dislikes. But, granted a large widely read group in a school, the reception of good verse becomes something in the nature of a triumph; the public reading is listened to with a keenness that is felt, the approval is spontaneous and obviously genuine, the later chatter in hall and lunchroom marks it for its own.[1]

The drift toward the better book has been steady and persistent. We have no "lists," although we recommend to pupils and parents the booklet on reading by S. A. Leonard, a former teacher of English in the Lincoln School, whose drive for good reading at the very beginning of the school is still operating.[2] With us the recommendation of a book comes best out of the moment's need; and no hour passes without some necessary title appearing on the blackboard or on the bulletin boards. Regularly complete lists of the most recent reading of a whole class are bulletined for the benefit of those who wish to inquire of the reading of a neighbor.

Occasionally a class with an accumulation of interesting reading will take a period to tell one another of "something good." Professor and Mrs. Julius Sachs will recall one belligerent hour in a ninth-grade class when a boy sought to prove the worth of the then little known Katherine Mansfield, a difficult task for an even older critic, and how he succeeded in first arousing their disdain and then tantalizing

---

[1] "Why, they talk about poetry while they eat!" Visitor's comment, January, 1923.

[2] *Reading for Realization of Varied Experiences*, by S. A. Leonard (Lippincott, Philadelphia; paper, 50 cents). A very necessary pamphlet for pupil and parent, and for teachers no matter what the subject of instruction; the annotated lists cover all the fields of interest of children of all ages.

their curiosity to know more of her. In this instance, by the way, both *Bliss* and *The Garden Party* became eventually the most popular books of fiction of the year, spreading out into the high school generally, a fact which makes the whole problem of grade placement in reading a still more intangible mystery.

Book reports—brief notations on a card—are read aloud, the more significant being printed in the *Lore* and the *Lorette* along with those fuller reports that just could not be held to the limits of a library card. Samples of this sort of annotating in the elementary school are given in Miss Eaton's account of the Lincoln School library.[1] Here are a few types from the high school, some of which have already been printed in *Lincoln Verse, Story and Essay*. The Roman numerals indicate the grade of the writer.

BOOK REPORTS

(The oft-stated object of the Book Report is to convey, as briefly as may be, to one who has not read the book some notion of the kind of experience he will be likely to meet; to attract him to read, therefore, or to warn him away.)

Senior High School

The Story Teller's Pack by Frank Stockton is a group of pleasant, well-written short stories. The tales are fanciful, improbable though not impossible, done in somewhat the spirit of a fairy story. No particular effort is expended towards making the story or characters realistic, yet there are many bits of human nature. The whole style is humorous, a mild, chuckling type of humor, nothing uproarious. All in all, they make very pleasant reading. —XII.

Typhoon is a sea tale. It is not a yarn spun from the infinite and romantic imagination of some harpy, but as vivid and realistic a picture of a storm at sea as one may have with his two legs on

---

[1] *The Lincoln School Library*, by Anne T. Eaton, *Teachers College Record*, January, 1923.

dry ground and a steady chair beneath him. . . . One feels the whip of salt water in the eyes, the swell and lurch, the groping for something—anything—to grab to. One sees the livid, dirty faces of the Chinamen; one senses the panic and the terror in their souls. . . . The fascination of the book lies not alone in the depicting of the storm, but also in the characters. Interestingly, clearly, they are impressed upon one's memory, their inward traits even more so than their physical appearance. Indeed, as a character study alone, *Typhoon* would be remarkable. We see them all: stolid, unemotional to the point of stupidity, dutiful MacWhirr, yet with elements of greatness in him; Jukes, brilliant in flashes, young; Rout, snarling, cowering, almost a rotter. Everyone will find something interesting here. To those who have any love for the sea, or any desire to know the power and passion of the elements, to those who would be tossed and fascinated by it, to them, I would unhesitatingly recommend *Typhoon* by Joseph Conrad.—XI.

Home Fires in France by Dorothy Canfield is a series of war sketches at the front, or else very near it. All of them are uncomfortably real. In spite of the fact that the war is over, they give most readers a wild, unreasonably, nearly uncontrollable longing to go over and do something about it—something desperate.—XI.

If I May by A. A. Milne. These essays by Milne are patchworky. Sometimes one feels that he thinks he is being really quite clever, and again one finds a sincere piece. Now and then he gives a surprising flop at the last. However, the reader feels it coming, or hears the author saying to himself, "I'm going to make a clever twist at the end." And he does.—X.

The Harp-Weaver and Other Poems. It is cruel to review it. It is too lovely. Nothing can be said better than, "Read it!" She has a number of lovely sonnets and after reading each one you feel she has told you another of her secrets. The title poem is wonderful; or, rather, awful. It makes you think of all the beautiful sad things mothers do for their children. She writes of death, too often for one so young. I should like her to be quite gay all the time; she is best that way.—XI.

Cæsar and Cleopatra by Bernard Shaw. This play is a very amusing drama of Cæsar's exploits in Egypt. It is a very humorous contrast between the stony yet fruitful mind of Cæsar and the playful girlish character of Cleopatra. In the second scene before the great Sphinx on the desert Cleopatra is so young and girlish, and Cæsar is so dominating, that the contrast makes you laugh more than once. During the play you can see that he is trying to see if she perchance has an inner self more serious and conscientious. Often you wonder how much Cæsar really knows and how much he is bluffing.—X.

My experience with *Pilgrim's Progress* is probably rather different from the average experience, because of certain circumstances at home. Where I am staying there are quantities of beautifully bound books, such as Stevenson, Dumas, Shakespeare, and others, which, when I was about eight or ten years old, failed to appeal or interest me, but there were two books which I liked. One was "Russian Wonder Tales" and the other was Bunyan's "Pilgrim's Progress." I read these books chiefly because they had pictures. I remember "Pilgrim's Progress" more for the story than for the morals in it. I often wondered why the author gave the characters such queer names. I always have enjoyed the story and the pictures. When I read the book now I realize the wonderful work in it—the writing of a very serious and moral book in such an interesting way. After you have read it you sometimes see your friends and enemies as different characters in the book, so well are the characters characterized.—X.

JUNIOR HIGH SCHOOL

The Cruise of the Cachalot by First Mate Bullen is not a story, because it is true, but it is the best story I have read in a long time. It is written actually by a sailor who rose to be first mate on one of those old two to three year whaling cruises and is full of adventure with pictures of sea monsters and strange people of strange seas that stay in your mind long after.—IX.

When We Were Very Young by A. A. Milne is full of the funniest poetry by a boy named James James Morrison Morrison Weatherby George Duprey. Fathers and mothers will like it (mine did) and your smallest brother and sister, if they are not too small, will too. One of the best poems in the book is *Disobedience*, but you are always liking another best. The *Royal Bread and Butter*, I think the name is, is awfully good.—IX.

The Hunting of the Snark by Lewis Carroll who wrote *Alice in Wonderland* and *Through the Looking Glass*. I was quite surprised to learn he had written this book too, and I was glad to get it but it is nothing like the other two. However, you would enjoy it if you like pure nonsense verses done into a long story which seems to be going on frightfully fast and furious but never really gets anywhere. —VIII.

The White Monkey continues the story of the Forsytes into another generation but while the names are mentioned it does not seem like the other stories at all. Perhaps that really doesn't matter for it keeps you going with a story of its own. I did not care for it as I did the others. I couldn't get interested in any of the people but a couple of minor characters, a man who steals to save his wife from starvation and his wife who becomes an artist's model for love of the thief. They were wonderful. I couldn't get enough of them. I didn't care what happened to the other characters, and their so-called moonings over their so-called troubles bored me.—IX.

A Trip to the Moon by Jules Verne shows you how a scientist could really go to the moon if he wanted to. They are blown up in a projectile, aimed with just the right amount of gunpowder to blow them out of the orbit of the earth and on to the moon. In the middle of the journey they are attracted equally by the earth and the moon and so float in the air, the chickens they carry with them float too, and one lays an egg while floating in the air. A glass of wine poured out at this time takes a spherical shape like the earth. A dog dies and they throw it out through a trap door in the projectile and it begins to travel around the projectile like a moon. The men being scientists calculate its orbit. It is accurate scientifically and a good story.—VIII.

The Young Visiters by Daisy Ashford. I don't see anything in *The Young Visiters* so remarkable by Daisy Ashford. They say it is a remarkable book for a little girl to write and that it is very funny. It doesn't seem to me to be remarkable but very poor and it is not so very funny.—VIII.

Any one who enjoyed reading *Treasure Island* will enjoy *Porto Bello Gold*, which is a successor to this book. It tells of the experiences of David Omerod, a boy of about fifteen years who was kidnapped by a gang of pirates who came into the harbor of the town in a King's ship followed by another old sailing vessel. Their leader was Captain Murray, a rather old but stately gentleman, very richly dressed.

Omerod and his big Dutch friend, Peter, who insisted upon going with the boy, had a big adventure that will hold you until you finish the book. Murray captures a large Spanish man-o'-war and an immense treasure, taking with them the captain, a friend of Murray's and his daughter whom Omerod takes a liking to.

The best part and most exciting part of the story follows. What was Murray, a well-to-do gentleman, doing with a class of pirates so unlike himself? What became of the treasure? What was the fate of Murray, the captives, and everybody else?—IX.

Great Expectations by Charles Dickens. The plot of this story is a very queer one indeed. Miss Havisham was in her bridal dress awaiting the coming of the groom. She was prepared to be married but at the last moment the groom decided it would not be. This disappointed her so that she never saw the light of day again. She never changed her bridal dress, nor had the large bridal cake removed from its place on the long table. Pip, the hero of the story, has a wonderful fortune given him by an unknown benefactor. The outcome of this gift forms a very pathetic part of the story.— VIII.

The Lost World by Sir Arthur Conan Doyle is one of my favorite books. It is about the adventures of modern men in the lost world of a prehistoric age in South America, where the race of savage monsters, supposed to be extinct, still exist. Four men are alone in a jungle of horrors, entrapped and prey to beasts twenty times as large as one elephant.—VII.

Robinson Crusoe by Daniel DeFoe. This is the dullest book I ever read in my life. Through many many pages it tells only about the things Robinson Crusoe cooks and eats and makes on his desert island. All a child needs of this story, I think, can be found in the many short stories rewritten from it.—VII.

The Young Trailer is by Altsheler. It is about a boy whose family went West and started a settlement. He was captured by Indians, and came back and saved the settlement from hostile Indians. He also had many other adventures.—VII.

To give concretely the character of the outside reading, as a help to an understanding of the literary soil on which our creative work flourishes, we present below a picture of the "reading for pleasure" of two high-school classes taken on a random mid-winter day. To assure ourselves that each title represents a natural choice, the data have been checked by reference to book reports and library slips, and, where necessary, by thoroughly concealed oral quizz. Each pupil is represented by a number; none are omitted except those who were absent on the days the check was made.

ELEVENTH GRADE

(Last three books read this term, and book now being read. Taken December 16th)

BOYS

1. *All God's Chillun Got Wings* (O'Neill); *A Few Figs from Thistles* (Millay); *Carmina* (Daly). Now reading: *The Riverman* (White).
2. *Irish Fairy Tales* (Stephens); *Rubaiyat* (Fitzgerald); *Collected Poems*, Vol. I. (Noyes). Now reading: *Drake* (Noyes).
3. *If* (Dunsany); *If Winter Comes* (Hutchinson); *Justice* (Galsworthy). Now reading: *Gods of the Mountain* (Dunsany); *Land of Heart's Desire* (Yeats).
4. *Hassan* (Flecker); *If* (Dunsany); *Others for 1917* (Kreymborg). Now reading: *Henry Brocken* (de la Mare).
5. *If* (Dunsany); *The Pigeon* (Galsworthy); *A Kiss for Cinderella* (Barrie). Now reading: *The Emperor Jones* (O'Neill).
6. *My Friend's Book* (France) *On Reading* (Brandes); *Where the Blue Begins* (Morley). Now reading: *Pickwick Papers* (Dickens).
7. *The Mayor of Casterbridge* (Hardy); *New Hampshire* (Frost); *"—And Other Poets"* (Untermeyer). Now reading: *Looking Backward* (Bellamy).
8. Books I and II of *Paradise Lost* (Milton); *The Great Divide* (Moody); *Ariel* (Maurois). Now reading: *Pickwick Papers* (Dickens); *Little Pierre* (France).

9. *The Brood of the Witch Queen* (Rohmer); *The Spell of the Yukon* (Service); *The Three Musketeers* (Dumas). Now reading: *A Connecticut Yankee at King Arthur's Court* (Twain).

10. *The Vicar of Wakefield* (Goldsmith); *Van Bibber and Others* (Davis); *The Snare* (Sabatini). Now reading: *Vanity Fair* (Thackeray).

11. *David Copperfield* (Dickens); *Vanity Fair* (Thackeray); *The Vicar of Wakefield* (Goldsmith). Now reading: *Pickwick Papers* (Dickens).

12. *David Copperfield* (Dickens); *A Tramp Abroad* (Twain); *Stalky & Co.* (Kipling). Now reading: *The Scarlet Pimpernel* (Orczy).

13. *The Vicar of Wakefield* (Goldsmith); *Hunters of the North* (Stefansson); *Enoch Arden* (Tennyson). Now reading: *The Slave Ship* (Johnson).

14. *The Hand of Ethelberta* (Hardy); *Two on a Tower* (Hardy); *From Immigrant to Inventor* (Pupin). Now reading: *The Oregon Trail* (Parkman).

15. *Mr. Britling Sees It Through* (Wells); *The White Company* (Doyle); *Travels with a Donkey* (Stevenson). Now reading: Nothing.

16. *The Scarlet Letter* (Hawthorne); *The House of the Seven Gables* (Hawthorne); *Green Mansions* (Hudson). Now reading: *Hamlet* (Shakespeare).

17. *Macbeth* (Shakespeare); *Richard II* (Shakespeare); *Fables* (Æsop). Now reading: *Fairy Tales* (Grimm).

18. *The Tempest* (Shakespeare); *Pickwick Papers* (Dickens); *Fighting Back* (Wittwer). Now reading: Nothing.

19. *Captains Courageous* (Kipling); *She Blows!* (Hopkins); *Fourteen Years a Sailor* (Kenlon), Now reading: *The Boy Whaler* (Tucker).

20. *Danger* (Doyle); *The Knight on Wheels* (Hay); *Blind* (Poole). Now reading: Nothing.

21. *The Sea Hawk* (Sabatini); *Twenty Years After* (Dumas); *The Viscount of Bragelonne* (Dumas). Now reading: Nothing.

22. *Haunch, Paunch, and Jowl* (Anon.); *The Viscount of Bragelonne* (Dumas); *Typhoon* (Conrad). Now reading: Nothing.

23. *The Pathfinder* (Cooper); *A Tale of Two Cities* (Dickens);

The Sea Rover (Cooper). Now reading: *The House Boat on the Styx* (Bangs).

24. *The World Set Free* (Wells); *Luck on the Wing* (Haslet); *The Daredevil of the Army* (Corcoran). Now reading: *Ballads* (Service).

GIRLS

1. *The Nigger of the Narcissus* (Conrad); *Typhoon* (Conrad); *The Four Horsemen* (Ibáñez). Now reading: *The Snow Man* (Sand).

2. *Les Misérables* (Hugo); *Island Nights Entertainment* (Stevenson); *The Crock of Gold* (Stephens). Now reading: *An Inland Voyage* (Stevenson).

3. *Concerning Paul and Fiammetta* (Harker); *The Heart of a Dog* (Terhune); *Treve* (Terhune). Now reading: *Jim Davis* (Masefield).

4. *To Tell You the Truth* (Merrick); *The Tryst* (Merrick); *The Quohaug* (Lincoln). Now reading: *The Real Lincoln* (Weik).

5. *Captain Blood* (Sabatini); *The Man Without a Country* (Hale); *Tom Sawyer* (Twain). Now reading; *Letters to His Children* (Roosevelt).

6. *Cranford* (Gaskell); *Pride and Prejudice* (Austen); *Essays of Elia* (Lamb). Now reading: *Ariel* (Maurois).

7. *Vanity Fair* (Thackeray); *Auld Licht Idylls* (Barrie); *The Green Hat* (Arlen). Now reading: *Autobiography* (Twain).

8. *General William Booth Enters into Heaven* (Lindsay); *The Dark Forest* (Walpole); *The Chinese Nightingale* (Lindsay). Now reading: *A Tramp Abroad* (Twain).

9. *American Poetry Since 1900* (Untermeyer); *Pictures of the Floating World* (Lowell); *The Hound of Heaven* (Thompson). Now reading: *Henry Esmond* (Thackeray); *Tess of the d'Urbervilles* (Hardy).

10. *The Garden of Folly* (Leacock); *The Pigeon* (Galsworthy); *A Lost Lady* (Cather). Now reading: *Dauber* (Masefield).

11. *Julie Cain* (O'Higgins); *Elsie and the Child* (Bennett). Now reading: *Henry Esmond* (Thackeray).

12. *The Able McLaughlins* (Wilson); *The Life of Oliver Goldsmith* (Irving); *The Silver Forest* (Williams). Now reading: *The New Morning* (Noyes).

13. *The Woman of Knockaloe* (Cain); *The Forest Lovers* (Hewlett); *Pride and Prejudice* (Austen). Now reading: *Ariel* (Maurois); *Nocturne* (Swinnerton).

14. *Nocturne* (Swinnerton); *A Lost Lady* (Cather); *The Pigeon* (Galsworthy). Now reading: *Hassan* (Flecker); *The White Monkey* (Galsworthy).

15. *Tubal Cain* (Hergesheimer); *Justice of the Duke* (Sabatini). Now reading: *Life of Cesare Borgia* (Sabatini); *Fraternity* (Galsworthy).

16. *Captain Blood* (Sabatini); *The Honorable Peter Sterling* (Ford); *The Three Musketeers* (Dumas). Now reading: *Our Mutual Friend* (Dickens).

17. *New Hampshire* (Frost); *A Boy's Will* (Frost); *The Light Guitar* (Guiterman). Now reading: *My Unknown Chum* (Fairbanks).

18. *The Crime of Sylvester Bonnard* (France); *Tess of the d'Urbervilles* (Hardy); *His Children's Children* (Train). Now reading: *David Copperfield* (Dickens).

19. *The Shadow Line* (Conrad); *The Thirteen Travellers* (Walpole); *Sentimental Tommy* (Barrie). Now reading: *The Life of Francis Place* (Wallas); *Shelley* (Thompson).

NINTH GRADE

(Last three books read this term and book now being read. Taken January 18)

BOYS

1. *She Blows!* (Hopkins); *The Cruise of the Cachalot* (Bullen); *The Spy* (Cooper). Now reading: *Two Years Before the Mast* (Dana).

2. *The Virginian* (Wister); *The Sun of Quebec* (Altsheler); *In the Fog* (Davis). Now reading: *Free Rangers* (Altsheler).

3. *The Prairie* (Cooper); *The Pathfinder* (Cooper); *The Spy* (Cooper). Now reading: *Twenty Thousand Leagues Under the Sea* (Verne); *The Talisman* (Scott).

4. *Two Years Before the Mast* (Dana); *The Boy Whaleman* (Tucker); *Letters from a Radio Engineer to His Son* (Mills). Now reading: *Story of a Bad Boy* (Aldrich).

5. *Fifty Years a Journalist* (Stone); *Life and Letters of J. J. Pulitzer* (Seitz); *The Rover* (Conrad). Now reading: *Autobiography* (Twain).

6. *South Sea Tales* (London); *Donovan Pasha* (Parker); *Salthaven* (Jacobs). Now reading: *Porto Bello Gold* (Smith); *David Copperfield* (Dickens).

7. *Possessed* (Moffett); *So Big* (Ferber); *Isle of Thorns* (Smith). Now reading: *Seventeen* (Tarkington).

8. *A Trip to the Moon* (Verne); *The Wreckers* (Stevenson); *Red Fox* (Roberts). Now reading: *The Black Arrow* (Stevenson).

9. *Great Expectations* (Dickens); *Old Curiosity Shop* (Dickens) *Bulldog Drummond* (McNeile). Now reading: *Blue Tiger* (Caldwell).

10. *Around the World in Eighty Days* (Verne); *The Lost Hunters* (Altsheler); *The Prowler* (Choen). Now reading: *Three Men in a Boat* (Jerome).

11. *The Final War* (Tracy); *The Great Mogul* (Tracy); *The Wings of the Morning* (Tracy). Now reading: *The Captain of the Kansas* (Tracy).

12. *The Spirit of the Border* (Grey); *To the Last Man* (Grey); *The Young Pitcher* (Grey). Now reading: Nothing.

13. *Three Men in a Boat* (Jerome); *Ransom's Folly* (Davis); *The Biography of a Grizzly* (Seton). Now reading: *Captain Blood* (Sabatini).

14. *Twenty Thousand Leagues Under the Sea* (Verne); *Great Pirates* (Finger); *The Old Soak's History of the World* (Marquis). Now reading: *Three Men in a Boat* (Jerome).

15. *Pearl Lagoon* (Nordhoff); *Whelps of the Wolf* (Marsh); *Lords of the Wild* (Altsheler). Now reading: Nothing.

16. *Sunset Ranch* (Cody); *The Last of the Mohicans* (Cooper); *The Spy* (Cooper). Now reading: *Mates of the Tangle* (McKishnie).

GIRLS

1. *Monsieur Beaucaire* (Tarkington); *Lorna Doone* (Blackmore); *Little Boy Lost* (Hudson). Now reading: *Tom Sawyer* (Twain); *Autobiography* (Twain).

2. *The Little French Girl* (Sedgwick); *Robin* (Burnett); *Ariel* (Maurois). Now reading: *The White Monkey* (Galsworthy).

3. *The Fruit of the Tree* (Wharton); *Hard Pressed* (White); *The Lengthened Shadow* (Locke). Now reading: *The Slave of Silence* (White).

4. *The White Monkey* (Galsworthy); *The Green Hat* (Arlen); *The Old Ladies* (Walpole). Now reading: Nothing.

5. *Ramona* (Jackson); *Charis Sees it Through* (Widdemer); *The Little French Girl* (Sedgwick). Now reading: *You're Only Young Once* (Widdemer).

6. *A Bow of Orange Ribbon* (Barr); *The Little White Bird* (Barrie); *Peter and Wendy* (Barrie). Now reading: *Jane Eyre* (Brontë).

7. *Rainbow Valley* (Montgomery); *Fidelis* (Abbott); *Ramona* (Jackson). Now reading: *The Count of Monte Cristo* (Dumas).

8. *Buff* (Terhune); *Bruce* (Terhune); *The Story of Mankind* (Van Loon). Now reading: *Silas Marner* (Eliot).

9. *A Bow of Orange Ribbon* (Barr); *The Maid of Maiden Lane* (Barr); *The Home Maker* (Canfield). Now reading: *Tennessee Shad* (Johnston).

10. *Nicholas* (Moore); *The Prince and the Pauper* (Twain); *Tom Playfair* (Finn). Now reading: *A Tale of Two Cities* (Dickens).

11. *The Hunting of the Snark* (Carroll); *Powder, Patches, and Patty* (Knipe); *David Balfour* (Stevenson). Now reading, *Crimson Patch* (Seaman).

UNSUPERVISED READING

Percentile distribution of eight hundred titles of books read outside of class by senior and junior high-school pupils

BOOKS OF INTEREST PRIMARILY TO CHILDREN

GRADES	VII	VIII	IX	X	XI	XII
Juveniles of distinction (*Lad, a Dog, Bob, Son of Battle, Treasure Island, Little Women, Kari the Elephant, The Jungle Book, Tennessee Shad, Jim Davis,* for example)	.26	.16	.13	.04	.02	—
Juveniles purely (*Free Rangers, The Rover Boys, The Campfire Girls,* for example)	.30	.13	.15			

BOOKS OF INTEREST PRIMARILY TO ADULTS

GRADES	VII	VIII	IX	X	XI	XII
Standard authors: to Kipling	.15	.10	.25	.37	.30	.19
Standard authors: from Kipling on (Kipling, Masefield, Conrad, Shaw, Barrie, Synge, Stevenson, Moody, O'Neill, Frost, for example)	.14	.20	.17	.25	.36	.32
Contemporary writers of consequence (Poole, Merrick, Cather, Train, Walpole, Morley, Stevens, for example)	.06	.29	.23	.28	.27	.46
Commonplace adult fiction (The Lone Horseman of the Pampas, The Middlemarsh Mystery, The Purple Fan are type titles)	.09	.12	.07	.06	.05	.03
	1.00	1.00	1.00	1.00	1.00	1.00

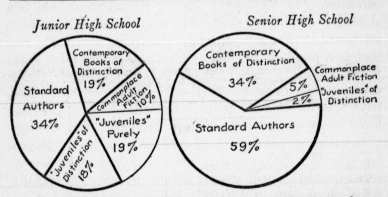

Junior High School   Senior High School

A random selection of eight hundred titles of books read outside of class discloses a high standard of reading-for-interest: in the Junior High School 71% and in the Senior High School 95% may be classified as books of distinction.

A further note must be added, if a true understanding is to be had of the causes that lead our pupils to desire to read widely and well.   As we have no prescribed "lists," so we make no restrictions on the kind of book that may be read. In the battle of the books we take neither the side of the ancients nor of the moderns.   Naturally enough, we make clear the necessity for reading some of the books known generally by the world of cultivated persons, an easy argument to prove; and we invite our pupils, aside from other standards, to test out the utility of any piece of reading for its worth as a passport to the regions of our equals and our betters.   That is simply a matter of common sense.   Any high-school pupil may be led to see the necessity of having some actual reading experience with, say, the *Odyssey*, if for no other reason than that he must be able to understand later references to it.   In that sense one is more sure of the future value of *Hamlet* than of the latest serial in the most approved monthly; and, in a similar way, one could make a case for *An Essay on Comedy and the Uses of the Comic Spirit* as against *The Middletown Mystery* merely on its use as a shibboleth to an even more select intellectual circle, if one is interested in that sort of thing.   And it is conceivable, too, that to a pupil of the upper high-school grades some books would assume a high practical value on account, almost solely, of their use as preparation for college.   These aspects have been in mind, no doubt, in choosing some of the titles listed above under "Unsupervised Reading."

However, we try to keep open-minded even here.   Browning may be a better poet to know than Masefield, but we refuse to hold a brief for either against the other.   Judicially, when questioned, we state such facts as are known, but it is important for us in all our relationships with our pupils that we should not even seem to hold up a prisms-and-prunes standard.   We try to remember that thirty years and more ago the pedagogues of the period were classifying *Huckleberry Finn* derisively with *Peck's Bad Boy;* and the *Fables in Slang* were not then to be mentioned at all.   No; we must be in the position to welcome any honest delight of our pupils, and know that if there is, as we believe, a stairway of literary taste leading upward to finer air and more beautiful vistas, it is built out of pages of every known kind of reading matter from *The Rover Boys* through *Deadwood Dick* and *The Lone Horseman of the Pampas*, from *Betty Wales* through *The Sheik* and *How She Loved Him*.

> Every gaudy color
> Is a bit of truth,

sings wise young Nathalia Crane. So we have no sneer for any book that any pupil really cares for. The school, from our point of view, is not setting up the kind of literary delight that children shall be allowed to have; rather, it is seeking, with a wary eye on our own prejudices, to discover what those delights really are.

All this to emphasize the fact that the type of books disclosed in this random cross-section of the reading of our high-school pupils is especially noteworthy, in that we are conscious of forcing no one's taste in the matter through a school-teachery appeal to authority, or even to affection.

But we do admit to placing, right in their path, a cleverly stocked and cleverly arranged school library, of which more at length.

XI. The School Library

THE ingredients that make up the school environment, which, we believe, has brought forth the latent literary abilities of our pupils, cannot be adequately analyzed without taking into account the unobtrusive but persistent part played by the school library. Organized and managed by a trained librarian, it functions as a part of the instructional scheme, fitting so snugly into all the book needs of the school that no department and no grade is without some constant and continuous relation to it.[1]

The first thing, probably, that the new teacher in this school notices is the unsolicited "flow" of books and materials into his classroom. An interest which he has started is reflected instantly in the library and is there noted for such use as may appear. This is because the pupils have become accustomed to go immediately to the library to find out what they need to know; therefore the librarian is able instantly to detect the difference between an isolated inquiry and something that begins to take on the appearance of a mass interest. Within a day or two the librarian will know, further, whether the general interest is merely momentary— a useful but passing flare like, say, the folklore inquiries aroused by the visit to the school of a delegation of Pueblo Indians, or a slowly developing movement like the demand for contemporary verse a year ago, which held one group for six months and percolated right and left into other parts of the school.

In the first phases of class interest a small line of books, stacked for easy inspection, will appear on the loan desk. Later, if the call continues, the line will include other books and attractive pictures and quotations will grace the library bulletin boards. As sensitively as an expert broker knows the feel of the tape, the library now responds to probable future demands: with borrowings from other libraries of books, pictures, magazines; with strange volumes out of the librarian's personal store; with bulletin-board announcements of events of pertinent appeal—a public reading by Edna St. Vincent Millay (which, by the way, the whole senior class eventually attended!), reviews of the London production of *Hassan*, historic costume designs for a forthcoming play, and

[1] *The Lincoln School Library*, by Anne T. Eaton, *Teachers College Record*, January, 1923, for a fuller account of the school library, especially in its relations with departments of the school other than English.

so on, with delighting variety. By this time, granted that the impulse along the particular line has persisted and has become general, the small line of books on the loan desk has grown into a complete special shelf with its own library label; new books have been bought; supplementary material appears in the wall cases, and illustrations flourish under the plate glass of the exhibition tables.

Then one day the librarian appears in the classroom, almost invariably at the persistent invitation of some of the pupils; she is welcomed by the class as one having the same interests, by the teacher as a fellow conspirator! Perhaps she will have with her some alluringly appropriate material, Walter de la Mare's *Flora*, for instance, poems done to illustrate the drawings of Pamela Bianco; or it might be the very latest book of their favorite poet, Robert Frost, or the much heralded poems of Katherine Mansfield, whose prose had delighted and mystified them and whose death had come suddenly as a something sadly personal. We make much of her visit, knowing the compliment thus paid out of her busy hours; and we take on a renewed spirit, for we know that when the librarian comes among us thus personally we are no longer drifting in a shore eddy, but are on a strong carrying tide with the trades at our back!

The "flow" between the library and the classroom, whose varying degrees we have just noted, is indispensable for an understanding of the naturalness of our interest in poetry. A mother of a boy has just told me, "I rejoice that the Lincoln School has made poetry one of the manly sports. My boy and his boy friends talk and dispute over poetry as they would over any other natural healthy interest." My strong suspicion, and perhaps I say it who shouldn't, is that the library has helped to take poetry out of the classroom and so save it, to use Amy Lowell's bitter phrase, from that "drying and freezing process which goes by the name of education."

AN EXAMPLE OF FOLLOW-UP FROM THE LIBRARY BULLETIN BOARD

THESE BOOKS, WHICH WERE AMONG THOSE MENTIONED FRIDAY IN THE ELEVENTH GRADE ENGLISH CLASS "BOOK REVIEW DAY," ARE IN THE SCHOOL LIBRARY

(or *else have been ordered and will soon be there*)

Garland	Son of the Middle Border
Roosevelt	Letters to His Children
Brontë	Jane Eyre
Davis	Soldiers of Fortune (We shall have this later; meanwhile we have his *Gallagher and Other Stories* and *The King's Jackal* and *White Mice*)
Cooper	The Last of the Mohicans
Barrie	The Little Minister (We have also *The Little White Bird* and *Sentimental Tommy*)
Wister	The Virginian
Van Dyke	The Blue Flower
Stevenson	New Arabian Nights
Kipling	Kim
Stevenson	St. Ives
Stephens	The Crock of Gold (Coming)
Austen	Pride and Prejudice
Kipling	The Light That Failed (Coming)
Andrews	The Perfect Tribute
Churchill	Richard Carvel (Also *The Crisis*)
Doyle	The Hound of the Baskervilles
Mitchell	Amos Judd
Warren	Twig of Thorn
Rostand	Cyrano de Bergerac
Dunsany	Five Tales (We haven't his *Book of Wonder* yet)
Merrick	The Man Who Understood Women (Coming)
Parker	The American Idyll (In the bound volumes of the *Atlantic Monthly*)
Stefansson	(We haven't *The Friendly Arctic* but we have *My Life with the Eskimos* autographed by Mr. Stefansson when he was here speaking before the School two or three years ago.)

XII. CREATIVE PROSE

IN THESE pages we have purposely made our emphasis upon poetry. This, however, must not be taken to mean either that we have neglected prose or that the method of handling is materially different. All of these poets write a good prose—story, essay, criticism—as we have illustrated fully enough in *Lincoln Verse, Story, and Essay;* some write exceptionally in either form; and many of our best essayists have not to our knowledge attempted verse at all. As a further illustration of the spirit of the instruction as applied to any type of imaginative writing, these paragraphs on "The Story and the Familiar Essay" are quoted from the former volume:

We insisted, simply, that the stories and essays (for the school magazine), no matter how imaginative, should come out of genuine experience; but the influence of the printed page—other and older persons' experiences and attitudes—told enormously against us at first. Pupils wished to write upon themes that had interested them in the writings of adults—murder, hairbreadth escapes, the conventional cowboy, journalistic slapstick—without realizing that imitation always falls lamentably short; or they dropped back upon the one form—debarred early by the pupil editors—that must strike all young persons as an original idea, the wild thing of horror which turns out to be "only a dream!"

Eventually our restriction told; the writers began to look about them. For that reason our material is mainly concerned with school and home life and vacation time, as it should be, for that sums up the larger part of the experiences which high-school pupils find time to have. . . .

Here, too, the method is writing and revision, many times repeated. The art of writing comes up for discussion, not as treated in a textbook, but as craftsmen talk when they meet and confer with one another. The study of sentence and paragraph structure, for instance, rises invariably out of immediate needs. When a knowledge of the principles underlying the art seems useful— unity, coherence, suspense, contrast, climax, surprise, suggestion, and the like—they are taught; but often, as is the case with all true artists, such principles are employed instinctively without the need of instruction. Certainly the method is not first a general teaching of principles, whether needed or not, and a later attempt to secure practice in their use. Nothing is insisted upon, as a matter of fact, but the effect of reality, the complete transfer of the feeling, the thought, and the ideals of the writer; but on the way toward that end we are often delayed by bad spelling, obscure punctuation, and other structural defects that demand instant remedy. And while we may stop to repair the damage, we do not even then lose sight of the object of the journey.

In the creating of any kind of literature, the essence of the matter is to maintain a nice balance between instruction and the work of the artist. Art may not be coerced, but it may be enticed; and for a surprising little price it will labor beyond the dreams of Egypt's taskmasters. Nor must it be benumbered by learning—the place of learning is another matter; nor, for any reason whatever, must it be denied its own expression, no matter how humble.

Artistically America is coming of age. This volume of school verse is simply a sign of the times. One of the poets represented in this collection, Tom Prideaux, has touched this theme so deftly in his *Adam*, published previously in *Lincoln Verse, Story, and Essay*, that by reprinting it here we may give an example of Lincoln School prose, and at the same time, present a picture of America turning at last to the arts after the necessary grubbing years of settling a continent:

ADAM

TOM PRIDEAUX

"Each tiny blade of grass was precisely as long as one's little finger. Each tiny bug that chanced to crawl on the apple tree was squashed. Hand work, too. Every bit of it."

"And who," asked Agnes, "had such patience?"

"The patient one, who squandered his care on the Garden—it was the Garden of Eden—was no other than Adam. He spent all of his time plucking blades and killing bugs until the garden was as flourishing as your Aunt Cynthia's back yard.

"One day Adam came to the realization that the garden should have a wall.   Lizards and snakes disturbed his nightly slumber."

"Lizzzards and sssnakes," hissed Agnes, shuddering.

"A wall of some kind must be built.   A flimsy one would undoubtedly have served the purpose, but Adam's mind did not run to flimsiness.   There would be a great wall or no wall.

"So, with this noble thought in his mind, he set about to find sufficient rocks.   Adam was not content with little rocks, and often he would spend a week moving some gigantic boulder from its resting place to the site.   At last, after many months of toiling, the stones were hauled.   Now came the greatest task, erecting the wall.   Mud served the purpose of holding the rocks together and it was an awful time Adam had mixing it to the proper consistency."

"I always have an awful time making mud pies," mused Agnes.

"After choosing a mammoth boulder for the corner stone, he proceeded to cover it with oozing handfuls of mire.   He depended, of course, upon the sun to dry the mud, and many were the angry words he muttered when it rained every day for a week.   At last the sun came out, but it shone so hot after its absence that the clay cracked and crumbled.   Can Adam be blamed if he felt discouraged?   The rain and sun had made the grass fairly jump, and bugs hiked up and down the apple tree in great droves.   But, despite all of this, Adam was not discouraged, for he was a most courageous man.   Singing as he worked, he spent half of each day trimming the grass and squashing the bugs, and the other half building the wall."

"What did he sing?" Agnes thought to herself.

"All went well for a week.   Things were being accomplished, slowly but surely.   Then one evening when he sat down to wipe the perspiration from his brow, he chanced to notice, for the first time, the setting sun.   The sky was stained with the most marvelous hues, and Adam thought how fine a sight it would be if he could reproduce them on his wall.   Thus came the first desire to paint."

"I like to paint," said Agnes.

"He sat pondering over the practicability of his scheme when the moon drifted up like a silver bowl and poured its liquid light over the earth.   Now this was the first time Adam had ever noticed the moon, for he was always sleeping soundly at moonrise and moonset.   He felt enthralled, uplifted; his hand itched for something.   'Ah,' he thought, 'if I could put my feelings on the wall.'   Thus came the first desire to write.

"The entire night he spent in making up a system of hiero-glyphics with which he might record those new and unexpressed feelings. At dawn the sun found him scratching queer experi-mental forms in the dirt.

"With reluctance he turned back to drudgery. All the day he felt discontented with his work. It seemed twice as hard as ever before. And when night came Adam had accomplished very little. The desire to paint and write gnawed his soul. He could not sleep."

"Silly dreamer!" said Agnes.

"No, he did not dream. Instead he invented a cement-mixer, a tree-sprayer, and a lawn-mower. The next day he was delighted to see how well they worked, accomplishing more in three hours than his hands could have done in four weeks. And that's how he found time to paint and write."

"Well, it's a good thing he thought up those things," concluded Agnes, "for he'd 'a' been working forever in that mud."

XIII. The Litanies of Youth

Of course, if young persons must be seen, they should, at the very least, not be heard; and it goes without saying that they should speak only when spoken to. A nice doc-trine, and comfortable. And good sense, too; for what has youth to say that is not said better by the elders? It was in the spirit, therefore, of time saving and efficiency that in the past our forebears have advised the young person to shut up and stay shut.

However, the general enforcement of the commandment to shut up has prevented us from knowing what youth could really do if allowed to speak on terms of equality with the other branches of the human race. Oh, not that nonage does not break loose—especially in urban America—and set up his caterwauling to high Heaven. The point is that he rarely does it on terms of equality; he is too aware in every flaming gesture that he is breaking a law; that, in spite of his loud laugh, his elders do not respect him. This silent condemnation—and his secret acquiescence in its value—acts ever to thwart him in the attempt to express his genuine self. Only when they are brought up fearlessly to be themselves, protected from patronizing adults, or when in their play they forget that they are inferior, only in these two situations does youth give us a glimpse of what is as yet an undiscovered or badly charted region.

The two child-poets of our time illustrate this point of view. Hardly had we got over our surprise at the clear young freshness of Hilda Conkling when Nathalia Crane's nine-year-old muse set us agasp. In the preface to Nathalia's *The Janitor's Boy and Other Poems*, William Rose Benét admits the right of the young poet to sit at table with her elders, but throws up his hands at any explanation of the mystery; for, keep in mind, Nathalia Crane is unlike anything in the way of Young Poesie that has yet happened. Remarkable as Hilda is in her own imaginative world, her work keeps within the accepted limits of childhood experience, like the early paintings of Pamela Bianco; but Nathalia has the wisdom of an ancient elf child. And it is that uncanny child-maturity that I wish for a moment to examine.

The Flathouse Roof, with its "my heart is all aflutter like the washing on the line" might have been done by Arthur Guiterman, Dorothy Parker, or any other precocious adult, but *Old Maid's Reverie* is quite another kettle of fish. Her first line is a spinster's autobiography!

I'm tired of mirthless mirrors and their hostile heresies.

"I'm tired of mirthless mirrors and their hostile heresies," cries that honest woman who would "trade an old maid's theories for a rood of Soap Suds Row" with its "sunflowers and the shanties" and the "horde of baby banshees"— especially the baby banshees!—who plans revolt, therefore, and would betake herself to a "disarrayed domain."

And shoonless dance the saraband in some assuaging lane.

(Assuaging lane! Think of it!) She would go there, this
unassuaged woman, "in a barefoot mood" and—here is the
astounding last line—

As one who missed the rubrics in the litanies of youth.

In her slender volume, a mixture of startling and ordinary,
Nathalia has achieved distinction in at least six poems:
*The Blind Girl, Prescience, The Symbols, The Road to Roslyn,
Old Maid's Reverie,* and *My Husbands.* These should give
her work a high rank among the best contemporary American verse. Consider only one of them, and the discerning
need no further proof:

My Husbands

I hear my husbands marching
The æons all adown:
The shepherd boys and princes—
From cavern unto crown.

I hear in soft recession
The praise they give to me;
I hear them chant my titles
From all antiquity.

But never do I answer,
I might be overheard;
Lose Love's revised illusions
By one unhappy word.

I sit, a silent siren,
And count my cavaliers;
The men I wed in wisdom,
The boys who taught me tears.

To some I gave devotion,
To some I kinked the knee;
But there was one old wizard
Who laid his spells on me.

He showed me like a master
That one rose makes a gown;
That looking up to Heaven
Is merely looking down.

He marked me for the circle,
Made magic in my eyes;
He won me by revealing
The truth in all his lies.

So, when I see that wizard
Among the marchers dim,
I make the full court curtsy
In fealty to him.

Now how, we exclaim, did such extraordinary expression come from a child? My answer is to admit that it is extraordinary for any age, but to deny that it is remarkable for a child. My guess is that hundreds of children have so expressed themselves, or might easily have so expressed themselves, but have lacked a channel to publicity. For note, that Hilda's mother, a distinguished poet herself, was fortunately by to take down those first exquisite child fancies;[1] and in Nathalia's case there was first the gift of a typewriter, then the fortuitous impulse to send a contribution to the poetry editor of a newspaper, but, most fortunate of accidents, her luck in getting her first verses into the hands of so discerning an editor as Mr. Edmund Leamy of the *Sun*. Any one of these happenings omitted and either poet might have produced vigorously for a few months and then have turned to other characteristic child-like play; and the astonishing product would have been forever lost.

The theory of the present writer that many of the so-called inglorious Miltons were born primarily to blush un-

---

[1] "Hilda tells her poems, and the method of it is this: They come out in the course of conversation, and Mrs. Conkling is so often engaged in writing that there is nothing to be remarked if she scribbles absently while talking to the little girls. But this scribbling is often a complete draft of the poem."—Amy Lowell, in the Preface to *Poems by a Little Girl*.

printed, led him in 1920, among other reasons, to accept the
invitation of the Director of the Lincoln School, to carry on
an experiment in creative writing with the pupils of the
high-school classes. The story of that five-year venture,
published now in connection with a remarkable anthology of
student verse, gives some proof that while the gift of poesie
may not perhaps be taught, some of the litanies of youth
may at least be preserved from the desert air of oblivion.

The Lincoln School verse is not the exceptional product of
an exceptional school. No; the Lincoln poets are serious
illustration of a faith that a higher grade of artistic achievement is possible than is commonly permitted by the schools.
They explain why it is that we do not look upon the work
of such distinguished young poets as Hilda Conkling and
Nathalia Crane—and Helen Douglas Adam of Scotland
whose *Elfin Pedlar and Tales Told by Pixie Pool* was brought
out in America last year by Putnam's—as the product merely
of genius, but rather, as a natural and appropriate performance which seems exceptional because the creative work of
other youth has not made itself known.

One must remember, in this connection, that age has constantly belittled youth; that, conventionally, the young person may not, without impertinence, be considered as having
superior skill, knowledge, judgment, or taste. Shelley,
everyone knows now, was put out of Oxford for thinking.
Yet the inner spirit of youth is as old and as wise as it ever
will be, lacking only the power to manipulate things, particularly word-things; and even here, it has more gift than
we commonly allow.

In poetry, at least, we should have long since become used
to the superiority of youth. *To Helen*, *The Blessed Damozel*,
Thanatopsis, *When We Two Parted*, of no mean rank among
the poems of the language, were written by boys. An
astonishing list could be made of notable poems of our own
day that were composed, really, by gifted children. Percy

MacKaye was a mere lad when he wrote the chorals to his father's *Columbus;* Stephen Benét composed *Five Men and Pompey* while still in the preparatory school at Summerville, Georgia; Edna Millay's *Renascence*, exquisite in contemporary American poetry, was already a printed book when the author was just turning from her teens. Poets have always been free spirits; creative youth therefore never, never, never shall be slaves—even to Time.

XIV. TRADITION AND THE NEXT STEP

FROM the hundreds of sympathetic teachers who have come from far and near to watch us at work and to help us with suggestion, the most common remark is that our materials and our methods are so different from the prescribed English course in their schools that, conceding our results in happy youth daily amassing literary wealth, such ideal conditions of work are not for them. The selections of literature which they most use in their classes, they claim, are decided not by an experimentation with the pupils' ability to enjoy, but by the adult's notion of what is proper, and the adult of a previous generation at that; grammar and the rules of rhetoric are studied as things in themselves, applicable on a given scheduled day to all pupils irrespective of known aptitude or needs; composition, in spite of much new freedom, is still held within the polite limits of prescribed schoolroom requirements. "We have an English Course," they say sadly.

We teachers are of necessity a tradition-ridden craft. The thing called the English Course was handed to us ready-made by the generation immediately before us; it is a liturgy and a catechism put together by diets and councils of the past, and bears beautiful evidences of the pious hands of other days and of the outworn ceremonies of another faith. For a half century *The Lady of the Lake* (published in 1810) has been almost a sacred book. In some elementary schools it was the only evidence of "literature." For the whole of the eighth school year it was studied word by word, memorized, scanned, and parsed. Final examinations were based upon it; entrance to the high school was denied to those who knew it not; and book companies were busy with edited texts. At one hundred and fifteen years of age the "Lady" is still with us. To be sure she doesn't monopolize all the period given to the study of our noble literature, but she sits comfortably at the side. She threatens already with Burke's *Speech on Conciliation with America* to become one of those reverent works once living in the world of men now found only in the schoolroom. It would be an act of impiety to remove her. "Respect the aged!" cried Kipling's Mugger. "Respect the aged!"[1]

But let us be fair.

The introduction of *The Lady of the Lake* into the English course represents the fine attempt some sixty years ago to bring into the classroom the best poetry of the hour. In the classroom it stayed, however, long after that hour had struck, reminding us of the special prayer for one of the queens of Henry VIII which, in one Cambridge church, still remains as part of the morning service. *The Swiss Family Robinson* is another survival (cousin to the Rollo books); and, in the classroom, much of the roar of Daniel Webster still holds over into a time which has learned to be suspicious of oratory. The schoolroom emphasis upon American literature, the good and the mediocre, is an echo of the post-bellum days, at that time a very proper sign of our overwhelming sense of nationalism. It was not, then, an overemphasis; it is now. Our grammar is the Lindley Murray litany of the late eighteenth century, a one-time sincere attempt to learn to use the mother-tongue with distinction.

---

[1] In "English That Works," *Educational Review*, December, 1924, Earl Daniels makes a spirited defense of the English course as an art subject primarily, and firmly opens the door to all the junk and jumble of odds and ends—including "civics" and "etiquette"!—that inartistic administrators have for years been putting into it.

"We study Latin via grammar," said Murray; "let us not neglect English." We revere this fine beginning of the care for the common speech; we still have the aim of our forefathers; we question only their instrument.

What, really, are we teachers striving for in the English Course? I speak only for the teachers of the elementary grades and the high-school years. Our first aim is to instruct this generation of children in the art of written and oral speech. Sometimes I am almost willing to believe with Professor Lounsbury that this cannot be done. In spite of our striving, illiteracy envelops us like a pestilence—even us. If our children would only get themselves born into the proper homes, and stay there in between school sessions, we might offer a feeble guarantee to show a result. And if they would only practise what we so diligently preach! All the world of fresh spontaneous out-of-doors conspires against our perfect utterance. We try to hold our flickering flambeaux of learning in the "well of English undefiled" —excellent figure!—where the atmosphere is characteristically carbon dioxide.

Our failure here should have been expected; but we are not quite failing. In composition teaching we are breaking mightily with tradition. In no department of study has the new note of efficiency been more productive. The whole country is alive to the necessity of achieving a practical result in "composition." There are more suggestions for reform than any of us can take count of; and surely every other pedagogue has written a textbook. Compositions on the "Progress of Art and Science" and the "Comparison between Tennyson and Cowper" are thoroughly obsolete; as are such titles as "Friendship," "The Pen and Sword," and "States' Rights." Our children write sprightly letters to flesh-and-blood friends; they construct real stories and print them; they keep minutes of actual meetings, report for the papers, compile a daily journal, write up the trade or profession that already has begun to call them. And, as we here prove, they write poetry.

No longer is the "composition" a worrisome task dug out of books, tinkered by sympathetic elders, sweated over until Sunday midnight and brought in with a gasp on Monday morning. It is now a bit of joy done in regular minutes of the school session. And it is done naturally, as you and I write compositions—first, planned and thought over, then jotted down hastily, scrawled in pencil, feverish with the impulse of creation; here no thought of good script, or spelling, or fair margins; the bounding idea is spilled out on the page in gross quantity, sprawling, illegible, warm with life. Then it is sorted out, crossed off, interlarded, padded, punched, caressed into shape, recopied with care, punctuated, spelled, paragraphed, and grammared. Now comes the kind critic—we strive to be kind—who praises with faint, very faint damns—the ugly word is Alexander Pope's— and gives the young author a glimpse of the long, toiling, joyful road toward that most fascinating of arts, the craft of the writer. If we are not pedants there is some hope for us with children; if we can write a pictured bit of moving English ourselves, we can fix them rigid with desire, especially if we can do it right before them on the blackboard; but if we have luckily published anything, outside of pedagogical treatises, we can have them dancing after us like a pageant of charmed vipers.

The main trouble with us is that we teachers talk and write in the style of yesteryear. Our letters, our contributions to educational magazines, our very talk, are grim, perfect eighteenth century. Children soon learn to write that sort of composition. Boys will compose Addisonian paragraphs on sunsets and landscapes, without really caring a tuppence.

Would you and I accept what they write to their chums? I quote from an authentic letter:

She's a pipin old man and no mistake and shes got a pair of lamps that would jar you some peach I want to tell you come over and get known.

This Don Juan hasn't a mark of punctuation to his name and no noticeable literary grace, but he has an eye for beauty. I happen to know that he is clever enough to write a correct school theme on "The Leaves of Autumn," but obviously his heart is not there.

Our second aim is to discover to this generation of children the make-up of their own unconscious utterance. I shall presume that we have given up the theory that we learn to speak and write via the analyses of grammar. Children who know grammar do not necessarily speak correctly; and many speak well who know not grammar. Good speech is a matter of the ear, a linguistic habit; and much of the beauty and effectiveness of language has nothing at all to do with the proper ordering of noun and verb. The vulgarest utterance may be at the same time good grammar and bad usage. Tone, rhythm, modulation, enunciation, polite idiom, the courtesies of gentlefolk have almost nothing to learn from grammar; and these are the meat and substance of the art of communication.

Nevertheless, taking the language apart and putting it together should be an exhilarating operation. It should be full of surprises. The phenomenon of "me" and "I"— two words for the same thing; of active and passive voice— two ways of expressing the same idea; transitive and intransitive verb—strange, inexplicable habits of words whose histories are lost in antiquity; the dative and locative survivals of older speech—all this should be as interesting and profitable as the study of our instincts and emotions. Grammar will not give us the fluidity of unerring utterance, but it should tell us much of our ways of thinking and make us conscious—if it doesn't make us self-conscious by coming too early—conscious of the form and mold of thought.

But even here we senselessly follow tradition. Only in your day and mine we discovered that "thou talkest" was two hundred years obsolete and removed it from our study books. May I ask the reader to conjugate the present tense of "talk"? I talk; you talk; he talks? Not so; that is a good old form, still used in special cases, and the invariable token of the book-taught foreigner. "I go to my house now. I take my book," he says when he means, "I am going to my house now. I am taking my book." The present form, put usually in a footnote as an irregularity, is, I am talking; you are talking; he is talking. Much of the fun of Hashi-mura Togo is in his book grammar: "I hear noise. I go. I look. It is my friend. He soups. He soups loud." Of course, he should have said, "He is souping." Grammars give as the regular interrogative form:

> Do I drink?
> Do you drink?
> Does he drink?

unmindful of the horrid suggestion. The prevailing inter-rogative present is:

> Am I drinking?
> Are you drinking?
> Is he drinking?

The same grammarians make much of a to-do over the agreement of noun and verb in "person." Their aim, re-member, is to keep one from vulgar error. It would be almost impossible for any one not a professor to name offhand a common instance of non-agreement in person. That so-called agreement is a very ghostly presence; it is a pity to fright very little children with it.

Nevertheless, the children are forced daily to recognize the almost meaningless attribute of "person" along with the dead abstraction of "objective case" in nouns. Again the aim is to save them from incorrect usage. (But they could not possibly make a mistake in the use of the objective case of nouns; and you could not. Even the professor of English could not.) We may be thankful, however, that the grammarian is not consistent, or we should have "case" and "gender" for all our adjectives; for, of course, you are aware that in the sentence, "Mathilda spanked her charming sister," "charming" is objective case, and, obviously, feminine gender.

Teachers, like other folks, do not always see things as they really are, the most difficult operation in all creation. When little Gretchen says, "My sister sings good," Miss Alice, of Room No. 8, is disturbed, as she should be; but she fails to see things as they really are when she admonishes, "How will you ever get along with German in the high school, if you don't know English grammar?" Miss Alice should know that the German teacher would have an easier time with Gretchen than with Miss Alice herself. "My sister sings good," is already three quarters German, "*Meine Schwester singt gut.*"

Our final aim is to acquaint this generation of children with the best English of the past, to thrill them and so transform them forever. And what is the best English of the past? Everyone knows that for the fifth year of school life it is Longfellow; for the sixth year, Bryant; for the seventh year, Whittier (because we are studying the quarrel over slavery); for the eighth year, Poe and Holmes; for the ninth year, American literature with strong emphasis upon the colonial and revolutionary output; for the tenth, eleventh, and twelve years, college entrance requirements. Toward the pre-high-school period and the first high-school year we act as though the large heritage of British literature were not English at all. While the American boy is held to Longfellow *et al.*, the English boy would be at home with Keats, Shelley, Wordsworth, Coleridge, Shakespeare, Milton, Lamb, De Foe, De Quincey, Blake, Arnold, Browning, Rossetti, Burns, Hood, Kingsley, Tennyson, and Swinburne.

And would the portions of Longfellow *et al.*, set for home consumption be the best English even of those writers? We should have *The Psalm of Life* and *The Village Blacksmith* —frankly doggerel, the English tell us; but few teachers even know the incidental music to Longfellow's Dante. Here is the prelude:

> Oft have I seen at some cathedral door
>   A laborer, pausing in the dust and heat,
>   Lay down his burden, and with reverent feet
> Enter, and cross himself, and on the floor
> Kneel to repeat his paternoster o'er;
>   Far off the noises of the world retreat;
>   The loud vociferations of the street
> Become an undistinguishable roar.
> So, as I enter here from day to day,
>   And leave my burden at this minster gate,
>   Kneeling in prayer, and not ashamed to pray,
> The tumult of the time disconsolate
> To inarticulate murmurs dies away,
>   While the eternal ages watch and wait.

We might have by heart *Maud Muller*—"simply bad," writes one critic—but we might forget to put into the language soul of ready youth the magnificent pathos of Whittier's *Proem*, that honest and melodious apologia.

Of Poe we would present *The Raven*, the mechanical *Bells* and the juvenile *Annabel Lee*, but it is not likely that we ourselves would thrill to

> The sound of the rain
>   Which leaps down to the flower,
> And dances again
>   In the rhythm of the shower;

from *Al Aaraaf*, whose publication in 1829 was "the birth of a star, set in the heavens secure amid the constellations where are Coleridge, Rossetti, Shelley . . . perfect if not of the first magnitude."[1]

These children of ours need no interpreter for *The Bells,* nor are they helped much by the stage business of genuine tongues of brass and iron, pealing an obligato to the teacher's dramatic voice. But aid they demand for *Spirits of the Dead, The City of the Sea, To Helen,* and the incomparable *Israfel* if we would draw them into "the region which is Holy Land."

I need not follow this thought further. The "best" of Longfellow *et al.* would be the conventional selection. Further, of American poets added, we make much of the styles of yesteryear (*Evangeline,* for example) and "poems distilled from poems," "the swarms of reflectors," "admirers, importers, obedient persons" that "make but the soil of literature," but we do not know the exquisite Lanier—unless we teach in the South. And we should not dare to select from Whitman; probably sharing the belief of those who do not read him, that he, the most non-moral of singers (that "*Gott bedrunkener Mann*") is immoral and irreligious!

Seeking the "best," teachers would never agree with this critic—John Macy—who writes:

Three volumes of unimpeachable poetry have been written in America: "Leaves of Grass," the thin volume of Poe, and the poetry of Sidney Lanier . . . to make an adequate fourth one would have to assemble in an anthology the finest poems from lesser lyrists, beginning, perhaps, with Bryant's "Water Fowl" and including, if not ending with, the remarkable poem published only last year,[2] "The Singing Man," by Josephine Preston Peabody (Mrs. Marks). And a beautiful book that anthology would be, for it would contain Freneau's "Wild Honey Suckle," Parson's "On a Bust of Dante," and "Dirge for One Who Fell in Battle,"

[1]John Macy, in a book that may not be ignored, *The Spirit of American Literature,* now to be had in The Modern Library (Boni and Liveright).
[2]*The Spirit of American Literature.* He is writing, of course, in 1912 and therefore would know nothing of the outburst of poetry that was to make memorable the next decade in America. We should, therefore, add much to his list now.

Timrod's "Cotton Boll," Stedman's "John Brown" and "Helen Keller," Aldrich's "Fredericksburg" and "Identity," Sill's "The Fool's Prayer," Gilder's sonnet "On the Life Mask of Lincoln," a score of marvelous little poems by Father Tabb, James Whitcomb Riley's "South Wind and the Sun," Emma Lazarus's "Venus of the Louvre," L. F. Tooker's "The Last Fight," a dozen lyrics of Richard Hovey; William Vaughn Moody's "Gloucester Moors," four or five poems by Edwin Arlington Robinson, and some other verse drawn from the younger rather than the older poets.

And all the while we Americans have not touched the great river of so-called "English Literature." The point to emphasize is that we have not thunderingly questioned the taste of the past, the traditional literary excellence of our forebears. There is another point, a corollary; we teachers of English do not know—do not know with the "thrill" —those symphonies of our mother tongue which range beyond the comprehension of immaturity, without which, as an aim of all our striving, we cannot move forward at all. Our loved literature is juvenile. Teachers confess it. "The poems that have most influenced my life," they write frankly to my constant questionnaire, "are *The Village Blacksmith, The Psalm of Life, The Bells, The Barefoot Boy, The Last Leaf,* and *Old Ironsides.*" This is an average list. I forbear to read that of the really depraved; it would include such naïve admissions as, *Woodman, Spare That Tree, The Old Oaken Bucket,* and such frail lyrics as *The Father of His Country,* which begins:

> He was our president,
> The first that ever run,
> He never, never told a lie,
> His name was Washington.

Our aim is to acquaint the children of this generation with the best English of the past, and to have it thrill them and so transform them forever. Do we thrill them? More frequently, we drill them. Do we transform them forever? Indeed we do. Staunch opponents are they of Milton, Chaucer, George Eliot, and Addison—forever. Somehow we cannot stop them from caring mightily for *Macbeth* and *Julius Cæsar*, for Dumas, Zane Grey, and the *Saturday Evening Post*.

We are a tradition-ridden craft. The hopeful sign is that suddenly we have become aware of that fact. Our eyes are opened. We are keenly self-critical, alert to improve; we frankly take the efficiency test to ourselves and own up to our failures. There is no more helpful symptom in all pedagogy equal to the gatherings of teachers dotted all over these United States every school day in the year and most of the vacation days, teachers sitting at school desks themselves, under the instruction of wiser teachers. In some communities the teacher goes to school one month in each year; and in those communities a current of fresh ideas is slowly but surely combating unprofitable traditions.

The glory of Ichabod Crane has departed, along with the tyranny and pompous cock-surety of his class. We are students now, learners, eager to know, irritatingly inquisitive, willing to change, tolerant, unbiased and determined. With these qualities nothing can stop us, not even the English Course.

Important as will be the work of experimental classes in which new and more appropriate materials are tried out, classes where the notion of the range of youth-ability is being incredibly enlarged—as, we hope, this volume illustrates; important and imperative as these exploratory classes undoubtedly are, the case for the country at large rests ultimately with the teacher at large.

We are moving slowly forward, but the fulcrum of the lever lies now, undoubtedly, in the schools for the training of teachers. Many of these institutions—fortunately the older and smaller ones—are hopelessly tradition ridden, with teachers unskilled themselves except, possibly, in a useless textbook lore; but the newer and larger schools of education, with their stimulating summer schools, are drawing the ambitious dissatisfied teacher from every part of the land. The college does not offer us much hope in even the near future, for its traditional emphasis is upon scholarship, which, alas, has too little to do with æsthetic values.

As to the better teachers themselves, the willingness and the readiness are there. They crowd into classes for self-improvement, at night, on holidays, and during their vacation time, spending of their slender store, doing their share in the forward movement toward a new spiritualization of public education. The length of the next stride, in the judgment of those who are most seriously concerned with the outcome of the free-school experiment in America, will depend enormously upon the power of those who, for the coming decade, have the heightened responsibility of adding to the personal equipment of those ambitious leaders among the teachers themselves; for we must never forget the stubborn fact that confronts us in all our enthusiastic discussion of things educational: the kind of school will always depend upon the kind of teacher in the classroom.

LINCOLN SCHOOL VERSE
1920–1923

LINCOLN SCHOOL VERSE

1920–1923

IT IS natural for me to feel pride in my poets. On the other hand, as I announced at the start, they were poets when I met them. I take no credit for my gifts but only for my discernment; and I have wished to express myself here not as their teacher but as their friend.—WITTER BYNNER: *On Teaching the Young Laurel to Shoot.*

SUNRISE

I'VE never seen the great sun rise,
  For then I am in bed;
The sands of slumber in my eyes
  Hold down my drowsy head.

I *think* the sun climbs up the sky
  And throws the clouds away,
Then girds her flaming tunic high
  And strides to meet the day.

Soft-touched by birds' wings is her head;
  Her feet caressed by trees;
She turns their leaves to gold and red
  And stoops to drink the seas.

                    KATHARINE KOSMAK.

BLOSSOMS

OH! A bud all green and white,
  Twisted like a shell!
Something strange will happen soon;
  I can always tell!

Leaves are crowding thick and fast—
　Stems are brittle things!
Grave responsibility
　High position brings.

Something stirs against the dawn—
　Is it bird or bee?
Or a purple-hearted song
　Blown for you and me?

VALERIE FRANKEL.

PRINCESSES

IN THE day they stand by the lake,
Rustling their leaves when the wind comes,
Tall and slim and proud;
But in the night they are princesses
Clothed in white robes,
Dancing to strange music,
Waving green draperies.

Long ago they were maidens,
But they were haughty and too proud,
So were changed into trees
By a wizard old and brown;
And only in the night may they go back again.

In the day they stand by the lake,
Rustling their leaves when the wind comes,
Tall and slim and proud.

EMMA ROUNDS.

WIND IN APRIL

OH, THE trees and the hills and I,
And the cool wind rushing by,
　Ruffling my hair,

Rustling the trees,
Fluttering into a mischievous breeze;
Oh, the hills and the trees and I,
And the quick teasing wind tugging by.

ELEANOR BARNES.

MEETING

SOFTLY it toyed
With the curled ringlets
Of the young, green grasses;
Coyly it flirted
With the young, green trees;
Now patting them on the cheek,
Now dancing away
And looking coquettishly back
Over one shoulder;
But when it came to the brook
It just spent its joyousness
In little puffs,
This young, green spring wind!

E. F. M.

RED MAGNOLIAS

I

CREAMY petals blushing on the outside crimson deep,
    As if the wind had toyed too much with them
    And dropped soft-spoken words into them;
Yet white inside as if that soul did sleep.

II

Tossing red mantillas in the air,
    Haughty señoritas, dancing, swaying;
    To the world's pleading saying,
"We do not care! Do not care!   Do not care!"

KATHARINE KOSMAK.

CITY NIGHTS

When the lights of the city are bright and they gleam,
　And the moon looks down on the level street,
I always dream the selfsame dream:
Of hills that are wide and of woods that are green
　And of places where two brooks meet.

James Flexner.

THE HEAD HUNTER

The big bull lazily flapped his ear,
There was nothing on earth could make him fear;
This way and that his trunk he bent,
Then all in a moment he caught our scent.

He spread in a fan his ears so large
And, trumpeting madly, turned to charge;
Spitefully spiteful my rifle spoke,
But the big bull's charge, it never broke.

Spitefully spiteful I shot again,
And the big bull bellowed aloud in pain;
Spitefully spiteful I shot once more,
And the big bull rolled on the jungle floor.

I gazed in awe on the fallen king,
And wondered how much his tusks would bring.

William Sargent.

THE AFTERGLOW

The purple shadows fall on hill and dale
　And breezes softly blow;
Rosy tints and golden amber pale
　In the sky above us glow.

The sun's richest glories are left behind,
   They sparkle in the stream below,
No beauty can compare, I find,
   With the evening's afterglow.
               BEATRICE WADHAMS.

BROADWAY
Night Traffic in the Rain

TWISTING paths of golden light,
   Among them ruby trails
That pierce the black and shining night
   Like darting comet tails.

Twilight

   Roaring, clanking,
   Sirens screaming
   In confusion;
   Pink and yellow,
   Shifting, gleaming
   In profusion.

   Above the deepening blue
   The stars blink calmly through.
             TOM PRIDEAUX.

GOLD

I LAY and looked upon the sunset sky;
The sun had rolled
Into a sea of glass;
The soft attendant clouds had passed it by
And what remained was one clear scintillating mass
Of gold.

I saw the pale gold, like a star's last rays.
The daffodil-like gold-dust of the fays,

The gold that ladies fair
Let sparkle in their hair
So dark-eyed princes from a foreign land
Might fight with sorcerers to win their hand;
Pale fairy gold.

Green-gold—mysterious, jewel-beset,
Which makes one think of great Kings, lying yet
Within a pyramid upon the sands
Of Egypt—green, sinister gold which sheds a baleful light,
As those dark almond eyes of Emperors might
When their uncounted years of rest are ended by alien hands;
Dark, greenish gold.

Gray-yellow gold,
In bracelets, earrings, ducats, necklets, rings,
Cathedral's vessels, treasures, holy things,
Down in the hold
Of a ship that flew
While the great waves rolled
And the wild wind blew;
Great lumps of gold
Stolen year by year
And dumped in the hold
By a buccaneer,
Till the drunken crew
Went to Davy Jones
And the gold sank, too,
With the dead men's bones;
Yellow pirate gold.

Nuggets of gold, in rocky dancing streams
That in the West
Lure men to follow tantalizing dreams;
To know no rest;

Sickness, starvation, never-ceasing toil,
Horrors untold;
And yet with bleeding hands they tear the soil
That hides the gold,
The gold of hardships, rocky impure gold.

Now red, red gold,
Giving a smoldering glowing light
Like candles for the dead
That burn within a church at night
So purely softly red;
The gold that three great Wise Men brought,
The gold of a star that smiled,
For it knew that the glorious King they sought
Was only a little child;
The gold of love, red gold.

Slowly the sky turned deepest purple blue;
The gold, like sails of galleons, slipped away
Into the land where our own night is day;
And I turned homeward, wondering if they
Who live beyond the ocean's edge—if they
Would see it too.

KATHARINE KOSMAK.

FIRE PICTURES

LYING by the fireside,
Looking at the fire,
Lots of things can happen
As the flames leap higher!

A warrior leads a fiery band
Down to a royal shining bark
That flies the flag of the Fire-elf Land;
And it goes sailing to the Dark

Country behind the Big Back Log
Where a host awaits in grim array.
For the gallant vessel of flame
Bears what to them is a hated name.
Then—there's a crash, as of a fray!
A great flame from the town!
And the Big Back Log falls down.

EMMA ROUNDS.

A SONG FOR CLEMENT MOORE

(Each year on Christmas Eve the children of the Church of the Intercession,
New York City, march with lighted candles in a gay procession to the grave of
Clement Moore, the author of *The Night Before Christmas*.   There they sing happy
carols and leave each a wreath.   The writer of this *Song* has been one of those
children from her earliest memory of Christmas time.)

DOWN the lanes so long and white
Come the candles burning bright,
For 'tis the eve of Christmas Day,
And, children we, a wreath would lay
Upon the grave of Clement Moore
Who wrote a tale of Christmas lore,
How Santa came on Christmas Eve
Gifts for little tots to leave.
Children's faces bright with cheer,
Chanting Noel carols dear.
Softly, silently falls the snow
Covering all with mantle low.

The last carol has been sung
And on the stone our wreaths are hung;
Left the cheering children then
The wreaths, the grave, the quiet glen
Where happy rests dear Clement Moore
Who wrote a tale of Christmas lore,
How Santa came on Christmas eve
Gifts for little tots to leave.

CHARLOTTE BAYNE.

LA POINTE DU RAZ
Brittany

Rock upon rock, crag upon crag,
  Piled by the unseen hand of God;
Tossed by that mighty giant hand,
  At the world's end, untouched, untrod.

Against those walls the waves dash high
  And boil around the hidden cliffs;
Lord, pity the poor fishermen
  Out in their little fishing skiffs!

How many, for a few small fish,
  Give up their lives on yonder coast?
Few pass that rocky sentinel
  Guarding his lonely, silent post.

ELEANOR FLEXNER.

THE SELF–DECEIVERS

So MAY we call that intervening age
When interest in nursery rhymes has passed
And, to the woman's chapter come at last,
They needs must stop before they turn the page.
From out their babyhood and childhood stray
And gather some forgotten habit, here
And there a little whim, and these, held dear,
They keep close in their hearts and whirl away

They seem to think of childhood as a time
Which must be overcome. Their only thought
Is to attain the heights for which they climb,
And for that carefree innocence give naught;
Until they gain their dizzy heights sublime
And find that carefreeness was what they sought!

KATHARINE KOSMAK.

THE PIXIE MOMENT

A MOMENT comes, just as the sunbeams change
From gold to red, and shining through the mist
Among the trees, thin as a baby's wrist,
A moment when the friendly woods are strange.

Hung on a log you'll see a fungus cup
Belonging to a traveling pixie who
Has hung it there to catch the dewdrops up,
When he returns, to find it full of dew,
He'll ask his brother pixies there to sup—
And if you wait you'll be invited too.

Around the stump of some primeval tree
Whose mighty limbs have fallen to decay
The pixie's twenty daughters you will see,
Who circle round the giant in their play,
But shyly turn to mushrooms, instantly,
If but they see you standing in their way.

KATHARINE KOSMAK.

A FLOWER REVERIE

At TWILIGHT,
    In the rose garden,
At moon-time,
    Fairies dance and sing;
Each elfin chime—
    Hear its crystal ring!

Sweet odors
    Of the blossoms
That fairly soon must die
    As tinted petals fall,
Float up into the sky
    And o'er the garden wall.

Shadow-wrapt
   The hidden witches,
Chanting, bend
   To lock with magic key,
The flower doors, and end
   My garden reverie!

BEATRICE WADHAMS.

DAWN

DAWN, like a maiden of the mist,
   Rose, clad in raiment softly gray,
   Fringed with flame and gold and blue,
As the Sun her garments kissed.

Like glistening diamonds, she flung down
   Dewdrops on every drooping flower;
   And iridescent clear she wore
The Star of Morning in her crown.

Past mountains, fir-clad, hazy blue,
   Past gray-white, wind-swept seas she sped;
   Till opened wide the gates of Day
To let the Maiden Dawn pass through.

VIRGINIA VORIS.

NOCTURNE

THE moon in the heavens
   Was silent and cold;
 The clouds that blew by it,
   Like galleons of old,
Moved slowly, sedately,
   As onward they rolled.

The stars of the evening
So far, yet close by,
Stared hard at the city
In silence, and I
Mused on the quiet
That reigns in the sky.

JAMES FLEXNER.

THE WIND IS A SHEPHERD

A Lullaby

THE wind is a shepherd;
He drives his clouds
Across a field of blue.
The moon puts her face up
Behind them now
And sings a song to you.

So, sleep, my baby,
And the wind will keep the clouds,
And we'll look at them to-morrow,
Me and you,
As he hurries them through meadows
And they lay them down to rest
In a field of blue.

KATHARINE KOSMAK.

SHADOWS

FAINT stars, dark skies, and clouds that smoothly sail;
Far pricks of light; the clutching hands of trees
Barring the sky; leaves chanting with the breeze;
A distant hound's long, moon-struck, cadenced wail;
The lifting shadows at their ritual dance;
The noiseless things to whom the night is kind;
The half-thought dreams that tumble through the mind
When standing dumbly in a star-struck trance:

These little things that saturate the night
Make shadows lovelier than the brightest light.

JAMES FLEXNER.

FORSYTHIA

ON THE edge of the forest a young tree stood,
Strong and sturdy, with boughs of gray,
And near it blossomed a cherry tree
Like a cloud of white on the first of May.
But though the sun shone fair and bright
And the song of the birds was gay,
The young tree longed for the blossoms white
Instead of his boughs of gray.

So the fairies took pity on the poor young thing,
Standing so sad in the midst of spring;
And they spread over him a golden veil
Made of starlight, soft and pale;
And every spring it greets our eyes
'Round the bend of the road as a glad surprise.

Forsythia, its name is told,
And its fame is as bright as its flowers of gold.

KATHARINE KOSMAK.

JUST BEFORE LIGHTS

OFT when the sky is cloudy
And it's just pouring, too,
I listen to my sister play,
For there's nothing else to do.

The room is dark—so dark;
Growly bears, I think,
And witches in the shadows hide;
In gloom they rise and sink.

The music chimes with the rain
  (I thought a goblin's head
Was popping out again—
  But it's just a chair instead.)

Why doesn't Mother come!
  And we haven't had our tea;
I wish that Anne would light the lights—
  I'm sleepy as can be.

                    BEATRICE WADHAMS.

DELPHINE

THE rosy clouds float over
  The hills of green
And meadows cool with clover;
  The robins on the terrace sing;
The snowdrops bloom—
  How sweet the dawn of Spring!

Over the soft dew grass
  Upon the hill
There plays a slip of a lass;
  Like the day she is fair as fair,
And she gracefully spins
  With violets twined in her hair.

There stands a youth not far,
  Handsome, but shy,
Shy like a twilight star;
  At last he calls, deep in voice:
"Delphine! . . . Delphine! . . ."
  She smiles—Spring knows her choice!

                    BEATRICE WADHAMS.

CITY TREES AFTER SNOW

DESOLATE yesterday;
Shivering branches violet gray.

At night the stars sent down—
In pity of earth's nakedness—
A part of their own loveliness;
Tiny gleaming star-shapes
Lent each tree a crown.

Humble bushes, graceful trees,
For one brief ecstatic day
Stood in radiant array—
None so beautiful as these.

That was just for one brief day;
Now the city has turned them gray.

                                EMMA ROUNDS.

THE GRASPING EYE

A LIGHTHOUSE light that came and went
Over the snow and ice,
A path of wet light, laying bare
The endless white some rude finger
Had smeared against the low gray sky.
Timeless the compromise of day and night
Reeking with gray, chill damp;
Timeless the compromise of life and death
In its cold atmosphere.
The fingers of the tide had drawn
With her the ice-cakes in her toils.

The rocks like fallen giants lay
With broken fetters on the shore.
Far out were ships.   I heard the dark
Calling in hoarse and broken tones;
And searchlights, jewelled with emeralds, paled
The inky flowing water.
A furry shroud around me crept
Like icicles to my touch,
And I, in fear
Lest I be chained a monster there
By the blinking lighthouse eye,
Fled from the twisted rocks.

FREDERICA P. PISEK.

HARBOR SONG

To Alma Mater

WHEN comes the time for sailing of a great gray ship,
  (*Listen to the calling of the mist-hung sea!*)
You'd think, when happy greetings leap from lip to lip,
  How hard to be a Harbor and to stay at home like me!

Even now a ship is leaving for a longed-for place,
  (*Listen to the waves in their ecstasy!*)
And when it comes back weighted, rich in silks and mace,
  You'd think that to the Harbor would come longing to be
    free!

But when a ship returns in the starlight chill,
  (*Silent is the ocean with its mystery!*)
All losses are forgotten in that one great thrill—
  A bit of my own heart is brought back again to me!

E. F. M.

UP FROM UNDERSEA

BELOW the sea in a submarine
Such wonders man has rarely seen:
I see the tide with silver hands
Ever washing at the sands;

I see a garden, bright and gay,
In which the fish and sea-maids play.
A storm is coming from the West;
.   .   .   .   . ;

See yonder billow raise its crest!

WILLIAM SARGENT.

DEEPEST MYSTERIES

A GLORIOUS cloud bounds through the sky;
  I follow and peer, far away,
Where the deepest mysteries lie
  Beneath a mass of gray.
Gorgeous courts and castles rare;
Many knights are resting there;
A prince his princess doth adore
With music never heard before.
Night comes; her darkness brings
  A host of butterflies
With brownies on their wings—
Then the dreams of night arise!
Hark!   A silver bell doth chime:
        Silence time!
        Silence time!
The oak tree bows low
As fairies go,
Floating onward—onward—
Leaving behind a nightly, silvery glow

I shoot like an arrow
  Back to To-day;
The land of my vision
  Is swept quite away.
Dreams fly fast!
The gray cloud has passed

B. W.

CURED: A BEDSIDE POEM

I MUST go back to school again,
For the doctor's passed me by,
And all I ask is a notebook
And a pen that won't go dry
And a math test and a French comp
And my pencil breaking
And a queer frown on the teacher's face
And his bald head shaking.

I must go back to school again,
For the call of "Left Inside"
Is a wild call and clear call
That may not be denied;
And all I ask is a bitter day
And the white flakes flying
And a broken stick and a cracked ball
And the umpire crying.

I must go back to school again
To the vagrant gypsy life,
To the barley broth and the old stew
That asks a clever knife;
And all I ask is a merry yarn
And plenty of work and fun;
And quiet sleep and sweet dreams
  When the homework's done.

IN THE HOURS OF DARKNESS

WHEN the night is cloudy
  And mists hang on the hill,
There are ghostly footsteps
  And voices, thin and shrill;
Nothing will your looking
  Show you in the dark
If the door is opened,
  But harken, harken, hark!

In the hours of darkness
  Thronging from their camp
Dark and ghostly goblins
  Flicker by the lamp;
Listen to their laughter
  As they flicker by the lamp!

When the rain is falling
  And the night is bleak,
Something moves the knocker
  And makes the hinges creak;
Sometimes on the window
  A waving shadow falls;
Sometimes clammy whispers
  Echo through the halls.

They lure you with sweet voices
  When you should be in bed;
Something creaks behind you,
  Something creaks ahead,
Something gazes at you
  From out behind a tree,
But if you look around you
  Nothing will you see.

In the hours of darkness
Thronging from their camp
Dark and ghostly goblins
Flicker by the lamp;
Listen to their laughter
As they flicker by the lamp.

JAMES FLEXNER.

WIND OF DAWN

MOONLIGHT on a wall . . . Ivy trailing, clinging,
Casting velvet shadows in the brilliant radiance
As the breath of deep midnight
Stirs its hanging leaves to free themselves;
Then, with a murmur of soft and careless laughter,
Presses them gently to the rugged wall.

Moonlight on a wall . . . Ivy hanging loosely, slackly,
As the chilly wind of fast approaching dawn
Seeks to wrest the limp strands
From stones once sheltering, now indifferent, cold;
Then with a tinkle of light, unfeeling laughter,
Swings them hard against the stony wall.

WYNNE FAIRFIELD.

PHANTOMS

NIGHT falls softly on the bay
    As the Ghost Ship sails o'er the bar;
A hero rides upon the deck,
    Cold and still as a distant star.

Long years ago a ship sailed out,
    Slowly it passed the cheering pack;
Now no one in the town will know
    When the Ghost Ship sails back.

Over the bay the Ghost Ship sails,
　A pale phantom of long ago,
And a hero sails her back again—
　But in the town no one will know.

　　　　　　　　　　　E. R.

THE OPIUM EATER

The initial
temptation

His days were drab and lacking zest;
A grinning devil did suggest
That if he sipped of some narcotic
Life would then seem more exotic.

The drug
evokes rare
visions

The lifting of a cobalt haze
Revealed before his anxious gaze
A swaying jungle bright and weird
Where gold and scarlet parrots jeered
While swinging on the living vines,
Each one a serpent, who entwines
His amber coils around a limb
And swings the birds that perch on him.
He beholding this delusion
Found himself in wild confusion

Fantasy
merges into
horror

When there before his inner eye
The parrots flew straight to the sky,
While the amber reptiles turned,
With narrow slit-like eyes that burned,
And slipped like oil on to the ground
Toward the man whom terror bound;
And when they reached his shaking frame,
Breathing smoke and spitting flame. . . .

However . . .

His days are never lacking zest,
For now and then an amber pest
Will calmly crawl into his lap
And settle down to take a nap.

But my untainted fancy pure
With inspiration can allure
Rare visions of most anything—
Yes, gold and scarlet parrots swing!—
But I can well discriminate,
And amber snakes eliminate.

                    TOM PRIDEAUX.

SKIP–SCOOP–ANELLIE

ON THE island of Skip-scoop-anellie
There is made every known kind of jelly;
Kumquat and pineapple, citron and quince,
Pomegranate, apricot, all are made since
Someone discovered that jelly-fish ate
Fruit from a fish-hook as though it were bait.
Any particular jelly you wish,
Lower the fruit to the jellyfied fish,
After you've given it time to digest
Pull up the jelly-fish. You know the rest.

                    THE LINCOLN IMP.

POOR PUSSY–WILLOWS

WHEN April
    Blooms a golden day,
When the sky is speckled white and blue,
Come pussy-willows,
    Silver-gray,
They cannot purr, nor can they mew.

Each pussy-willow
    Wants to cry
As up the long brown stem they creep:
They cannot play "I spy,"

Or weep—
Poor pussies, they can only sleep.

PIXIE RAIN.

THE SPOILERS

ONCE we lived in Fairyland
With mysteries on every hand;
We had a dungeon dark and deep
Where wicked prisoners we'd keep.

The loveliest Prince we had there, too,
With a beautiful Princess for him to woo;
We put her up in a tower stout—
And we were the fairies who got her out!

There was a fairy Queen and King
With palaces and everything!
And we had ladies fair, and knights
Who had the most exciting fights!

And then they went and spoiled it all!
They said the palace was the hall!
They said the dungeon, full of gloom,
Was just the closet in our room!

EMMA ROUNDS.

THE BALLAD OF A PHILOSOPHER'S PICNIC

I

WE LIKE to dream on a clear night—
    "Oh! Oh! My eggs are far from fresh—
"For we forget when the moon is bright
    "That flesh is grass, and grass is flesh.

II

"For when the sky is bright above—
 "They've baked hard stones in this rye bread—
"Then you and I will talk of love,
 "But all that lives is really dead,

III

"And life is only empty dreams—
 "Who drowned that fly in my amber tea?
"But we forget when the bright moon gleams
 "That all that is so, cannot be.

IV

"And when you think that bad things rout—
 "Oh! Oh! My glasses fell in the stream
"But I will quickly fish them out;
 "I see their bright rims shine and gleam.

V

"Oh! I'm slipping! Help me quick!
 "Help me!—Blub!—I'm drowning fast!
"Get that—blub! blub!—ashen stick
 "And save me ere I breathe my last."

VI

"Don't you remember!" his lady said,
 "You remarked ere you fell off the brink
"That all that lives is really dead?"
 She sat and watched him splash and sink.   J. F.

ON HIS KINDNESS

When I consider how my cash is spent,
Ere half the year, with no more checks to come,
And that my parent won't increase the sum,
Acting most grudging, deeming money lent

Unto his son a debit permanent,
Then asks a true account of what's become
Of my allowance, says I'm frolicsome,
Repeating that he's most benevolent.

I murmur a reply, I do not need
Either his cash or his benevolence,
So proudly leave his presence, until late
He calls me when I least hope to succeed
And gives me more than's needed for expense.
Ah!   They are served who do not stipulate.

PAUL M. HERZOG.

ON THE IMITATIONS OF WORDSWORTH IN EARLY CHILDHOOD

IT GOES careening through my weary head
In broken fragments, scattered here and there;
A word comes suddenly from out the air,
But just one word, one line, and then I shed
Great (figurative) drops of bloody red,
Trying to write the thing.   It isn't fair;
Some folks dash dozens off without a care;
When I start writing inspiration's fled.

That sonnet keeps me wakeful many a night;
I've tried to grasp it, but I always found,
Just as I got my pen all poised to write,
There wasn't any sign of it around.
But now I've got it down in black and white,
It can't fly off again; it's caught and bound.

EMMA ROUNDS.

THE DOOR STANDS OPEN

THE ever-passing steps went by our door;
We did not listen then, nor did we look outside;
But now the door stands open.

Some hang back, afraid to join the crowd that passes;
Some gather in the doorway and watch eagerly.
I am not afraid;
I am not eager.

I stand by the window and look at the faces.
I would know what life is, what the world is,
Before I go.
Those who come back are often sad or tired;
The stories they tell are not always pleasant;
Yet all who go out are happy; and they hurry,
Looking ahead at something just beyond.

There goes one now.   She almost runs.
And there come some who are returning;
Their faces are lined and ugly, but their eyes are wise.
Not all of them.   I see one coming back
Whose face is smooth and happy,
But her eyes are empty—foolish.
Why?
I will find out.

There goes a face like mine that searches for an answer.
What has she learned?   She may tell me.   .   .   .
But she has passed.

I see a youth whose eyes are fixed on something far away;
His is a face to follow and respect.
I lean out.   "Where are you going?"

The vague, deep eyes turn slightly.
"Just over there."
"Where?"
But he is gone.

Here returns a man whose face must once have been like
   that youth's;
His eyes are broken windows, and he babbles without sense;
What is this world that does such things to men?

There stands a man who watches those who start out;
He sees them drop unnoticed things of value
For which he stoops and searches in the dust;
He is one who went out and has returned
With nothing.

I leave the window and look about the empty room.
They all have gone! I cannot warn them. . . .
'Tis just as well.
Youth's saving gift, I think, is that it will not look,
And cannot see.

I take a last glance back and gently close the door behind me;
I catch a friendly hand that's half outstretched;
And I am part of the crowd.

WYNNE FAIRFIELD.

LINCOLN SCHOOL VERSE
1923-1925

LINCOLN SCHOOL VERSE

1923–1925

THE greatest thing in life, my lad," remarked the Captain of the good ship *Preach*, "is to devour cabbage, providing that you dislike it; ram your nose in the mustard jar if you detest the odor; and be a surgeon if the sight of blood nauseates you. Self-flagellation is a sacred chore."

"You are undoubtedly right, sir," replied the Cabin Boy, "but if, preferring water-cress to cabbage, the spice of hollyhocks to the effluvium of mustard, and the magenta of wine to the crimson of blood, I succumb to these delicacies, what then? A nose yellow with pollen, a body literally made of cress, and a heart aflame with old Madeira! Although a freak, I am a super-specialist on those Delectable Three. And where would the world be without the individualist?"

"Also," commenced the Captain, unfurling sail for a gust of wind, "where would the world be without a common herd? We must provide a neutral background to insure sanity and balance. Moreover . . ."

"Wait," interrupted the Boy, "why preserve a background? The parts of a tiger's body are all different, yet they cog in to form a magnificent unit. Why not allow each man to express himself and perhaps become a living hollyhock? He still remains a congruous and indispensable section of the divine Whole!"

"You are impertinent!" rebuked the Captain.

So the Boy sat down to a mess of cabbage.

—TOM PRIDEAUX: *On the Cultivation of Hollyhocks.*

163

PRELUDE

You sing a curious song;
At first, disconnected:
Still, a strain of music is there—
I wonder what *can* follow.

ELLA FOHS.

SPRING VENDERS

O, BLESSED be the venders in the street
That flaunt their jaunty splendors in the street:
   Violets and daffodils,
   Whirligigs and windmills,
    Bright balloons,
    Rusty tunes,
Doughnuts strung on spindles.

Yet, the doughnut-vender never sells his crullers;
   Just the odor serves to make the children sigh;
While balloons and toys sell only for their colors—
   The flimsy stuff they're made of who would buy?

No one wants the music or a flower.
   Who flings a coin to hear machinery start,
Or pays for blooms that wither in an hour?
   He only buys the April in his heart.

TOM PRIDEAUX.

WILDFLOWER

CYPRESS and the wind child
   Flying hither-by;
Moon-maids, silver touching,
   And a russet sky.

Bending ermine birches
  And softly shadowed moon;
Little redbirds singing
  Faery forest tune;

Golden water bubbles
  On a pool of blue;
Floating, floating lily;
  Floating opal, too.

Wildflower—this
I breathe from you.

BEATRICE WADHAMS.

MOON MADNESS

Moon Madness!
I have it as no one ever has.
I sing wild chants
And dance mad rhythms
To the witch light.
                    It is my God,
And it hears my prayers
And answers them   .   .   .
When I am lonely
And in need of love,
The moon comes stealing in,
And floods me with passionate desire,
Kisses me and holds me with mysterious silver;
Takes my soul away
To the far hilltops,
And brings it back at morn,
Leaving only a bit of my heart.

Some day I shall not come back
From
                    the hilltops!

More than all else on earth
I love the Moon;
Yet were you my son
    And it should be your desire—
I would give it to you.

ZARA MOXHAM.

INTIMATIONS

I HAVE not been here before
 And I shall not come back;
Why, then, is the dust trodden
 By a faint, familiar track?

PHILIP JORDAN.

DOWN THE NIGHTS AND DOWN THE DAYS

THE clouds that spurred across the sky
Were puffed with redolent wonder
And nearby
The hills were golden under.
He said, "Good-bye."

Just the last few rays in a sunset scene
And the clouds grown gray in the gap between,
He shook hands, stuttered, and turned away,
Not quite sure what he ought to say,
And the higher hills had now turned gray.

She thought:
    "Soon the moon will rise and bring
Peace more lovely, and wondering,
More dreamful than the sun has ever brought;
The moon will drive the shadows far away,
And make the night more lovely than the day;
(He has gone without a word—was there nothing he could say?)
The night shall be more lovely than the day!"

She stood still, straight and silent, and the cold
Black closed around and held her in its hold,
But soon the sky grew softer, and the night
Stepped back and left her in the moon's thin light.

It burst the massive shadows of the dark
But formed some trailing tendrils of its own
To crawl from out beneath the trees and mark
Which way its slim light shone.
It roused the sullen stupor of the sky
And made the night seem twice as high
As it had seemed before:
With blanched white face began to change
All things massy into something strange.
It took the ponderous mysteries of the black
And then with wistful hands it gave them back
More subtle, yet more searching than before.

Again he came through the moonlight scene
Sure of his welcome, tall, serene
And laughing.

She heard him come and break the charm
Of wistfulness the moon had gently brought:
His crunching footsteps burst the lovely calm;
And yet his advent was the thing she sought!
She felt his light and power begin
To clutch her hard and then sink in.
An impulse snatched her and she fled,
Leaving his shadow motionless, a blurring gray;
She fled, and laughed to see the moon still bright above her
    head,
Making the night more lovely than the day.
                                        JAMES FLEXNER.

THE PATH

I ALWAYS take the path and not the road;
I know not if it is the pond or if it is the trees
Or the great drooping willow on the island;
Yet I must take the path and not the road.

ALWIN PAPPENHEIMER.

ABSENCE

EVERY night I push my shade up high
So that the light from just across the street
    Will shine on me.
It glares blind-white, and hurts my eyes;
But if I close them—
    I can pretend it is the moon.

  .   .   .   .

Awhile ago the real moon
    Slid through my window and to my bed;
It burned even through tight-closed eyes—
I pulled the shade
    To shut it out.

VIRGINIA VORIS.

THE POOL OF LILITH

And a curse was laid upon Lilith that she should abide alone in Eden.—*Apocrypha.*

SHE searched among the waters,
Dabbled bare legs in the brooks,
But they were all so cold
And ages old.
Even the lake was not quite right;
She wanted warmth and light,

A pool that would reflect unchanged
Her glowing guise,
And make her smile
Its skies;
To hold her youth.
And laugh back lies
At truth.

She searched
And found at last
Her prize.
Strange how it cast
Her face in stone
And shone
So hard and brilliant.
Yet she must catch
The shining mirror to herself
And slip, a graceful elf,
Into the grinning bowl

Till, coiling here and there,
Her straying hair
Mingles with the pebbles
Fallen from the rim,
Fashioning huge chains
To hold her body down,
While little wrinkling ripples
Make a ragged sort of gown
As the luster in her eyes grows dim.

PHILIP JORDAN.

FIRST SNOW

PIERROT
> Shows off to the stars
To-night!
> In his spotted costume
Spotted white,
> Painting the skies,
> Gilding the moon,
Balancing pearls
> In a silver spoon—

Pierrot
> Shows off to the stars
To-night!
> Paling winter
In violet light,
> Spilling the spoon—
> And laughing to see
Pearl upon pearl
> Falling on me!

BEATRICE WADHAMS.

OH, SHEPHERD

Oh, SHEPHERD, free to pipe the days away
Shepherd, free to watch all nature play,
We, in cities, see only the leaving of the sunset
While you, the whole.
Oh, Shepherd, pipe the day away
Shepherd, let the whole world play!

MARGARET MAYO.

TWILIGHT

IF YOU watch in the quietness that comes after sunset,
When the sky is a candle-lighted bowl,
Before the earth-lights have asserted themselves,
And the fretwork of trees borders the gray robe of twilight,
A hovering drift of clouds slips into the afterglow,
And time is not,
And life-ties are forgotten things;
For it is the calm hand of God which has shaped itself so,
Poising above us.

ELEANOR BARNES.

WEARY OF MYSELF

MY TIME will come, but oh, how long it seems to me
Before the fruit is ripened on the full-grown tree,
Before the time when I may be what I am going to be.

LOUISE LAIDLAW.

TO TIMMY

WHEN we have laughed at life
And turned to hide our tears,
We shall see him standing there,
With laughter in his eyes,
To greet us
Who have traversed all the years
To gain a place beside him
In some earth-resembling paradise.

E. B.

WILDA

THEY called her "Wilda"
Because she was wilful,
Because she was wild.

And she grew up
  The way any young thing grows
When it is left alone.
I don't know why
  She always laughed
When others saw no joke
Or yet was silent
  When the rest were gay.
Surely she was human,
  But we did not know her way.

Once in a thunderstorm
  We saw her whirling down the path
And called to her—there was lightning—
But she did not hear.
Not one of us quite dared to follow her,
It was not that we were afraid,
Only she seemed to know something we did not.
And ever after that
  She would not look at us,
But turned away her head
  When we passed by.

Wilda, I was one of those
  Who did not know, dear.
I know now, now that you have gone;
And when I think of you
I do not see you any more
  A wild thing in the storm,
But as a sweet young poplar
  Baring its leaves to the wind,
With a pink cloud behind;
  And I hear a mandolin . . .
Sound of sun-rain . . .
  In the far off.
                  BEATRICE WADHAMS.

CLOCKMAKER'S SONG

BITS of rubies and bits of steel
Intricate brotherhood of spring and wheel
Ticking away on my mantel shelf,
Clocks that are ornate or pretty or plain
Ugly, unusual, ugly again,
Each one is mine, for I made it myself.

I oil it, and dust it, and love it, and mind it,
And I never, *never* forget to wind it.

Another Clockmaker, quite close by
Has a mantel shelf reaching from sky to sky.
He can make a clock in an ecstasy
Of wild, unbridled artistry
And set it down among clocks that are plain
Where it never enters His mind again.

And it ticks itself still on His mantel shelf,
For no clock is able to wind itself.

My mantel shelf measures five feet or more
And His is boundless from shore to shore,
But I make my clocks just as carefully,
And each has the same loving care from me—

And in this, perhaps, I am greater than He.

KATHARINE KOSMAK.

OUR MOON[1]

THE moon far coming in her misty veil
Parts wide the heavy curtains of the night,
Then gently touches grove and hill and dale
Filling the world with mystic, shimmering light.

[1]Reprinted by permission of the editors from the March, 1925, number of *Success*.

And now she spreads upon the sea awhile
The deep reflection of her cold, strange smile.

Ah, love! whose heart, so far away from me
Beats high in rapture on thy wooded hills
How strangely fair the maiden moon must be
As she stands thralled above those mountain rills.
To think—
This very moon whose rays here frost the sea,
In radiance bright, e'en now shines down on thee!

Louise Burton Laidlaw.

PATHS

To the Class of 1924

Paths are always winding;
  One knows not where they go;
One is always finding
  New nooks where far winds blow.

From a purple highway,
  Made smoky by fall fires,
They branch and nose and ramble
  Awakening desires.
Clear-cut against the burnt grass
  The brown pathway weaves
Around scarred gray rocks—like centuries—
  Under young and flaming trees.

Happy paths of spring-time;
  Mud-runny, oozing down,
Sucking at one's rubbers,
  Splashing on one's gown;
Leading 'round lichened stumps
  Where pale spring-beauties grow,
Where children watch for fairies
  All breathlessly aglow.

Paths are always winding
  About little hills whose tops
Look bravely off worldward,
  Past fields and homes and shops,
To a hill a little higher
  Which gives a clearer view
Of those windy, silent distances
  Where paths lead to.

THREE POEMS

FIVE O'CLOCK

SOFT and gray as a cobweb
Dawn hangs over the earth.
The green young trees stretch their branches
To hold it there.

ALMOST MORNING

The moon brings her opalescent fish
And lets them play awhile in the black water;
Then she gathers them up and takes them away
Lest the day hurt them.

APOLLO

All the world lay asleep
When softly you came,
Tiptoed, so as to waken
Only me.

Through the mist came your golden signal,
I knew it was for me
And I came out into
The morn with you.

We played among the green trees
And scattered all the dewy tears of night.

How short seemed our time alone!
Before I could detain you
You strode to wake them all;
You flamed and flung your fires through the skies;
The world claimed you;
You were no longer mine.

DOROTHY RAND.

YOUTH'S EYES

WARM and happy, starlit, love filled,
And more than all,
Confident . . .
   God—
Keep them always so!

ZARA MOXHAM.

YOU STAND ON A MOUNTAIN

YOU stand on a mountain.
Behind you the sun rises earlier each morning
Because it cannot wait to worship you.

You are outlined against the brightest light that men know
And you shine brighter still.
The glory that men need to live
Can only lightly touch your golden hair,
Bring clearer into view
The straight, strong, supple grace
The tiger's quickness, and the gentleness
Of a yearling buck in your limbs.

Humbly, adoringly, the sun passes over your glorious head
And when at last she must leave you for the night to love
She sends her loveliest light to where you stand;
And the rays of red gold

Deepen the steadfast purpose in your eyes
Warm and strengthen even more
The quickness and the keenness of your mind
And make the mystery of your heart
More unfathomable still.

And you stand on your mountain and look out, always out
Over the towns and Cathedral spires
To where the sea is tearing at the land
Impatient to kiss your feet;
When at last it reaches its goal
You will still be there to welcome it,
For you are changeless.

Sometimes you look up toward Heaven,
It is not very far from you,
And the inhabitants of the Holy City
Lean over the wall of pearl and call to you.
Sometimes you will look to your side
Where a wild bird will nestle on your shoulder
Or a doe with her fawns
Will nibble unafraid at your hand
And always find friendship and protection there.

But you never look down
For I am there, kneeling at the foot of your mountain.
From my heart springs a never ending flow of clear water
And I catch it in a crystal bowl
And hold it up to you
Until your radiance has absorbed it.

Then I fill the bowl again.
Day after day, year after year, I have knelt there
Looking up through the dark pines on the mountain.
I cannot see you.   But the forest is never dark to me

And the mountain is never unfriendly
Because I know you are at the top.
Aeon after aeon I shall kneel there
Offering to you my never ending flow of living water
And you will always accept it.

Perhaps I shall wonder, sometimes,
Whether, if my offerings ceased,
Your beauty, your radiance would fade.
But I know that they will never cease
And that your beauty is a changeless thing:
So in an aeon or two I shall wonder no more
And only hold my bowl more steadily toward you.

Some day a traveler will pass through the glade where I kneel;
He will ask for a bowl of my water,
Which is all any man would ask for,
And I will smile and shake my head.
He will beg for a little sip of it,
For no other water will quench his thirst.
But no; he must go away with dry tongue,
For my heart-spring will at last be dry;
You, who stand on a mountain, have taken it all.

KATHARINE KOSMAK.

IN A RAILWAY STATION

SHE sat there staring and then she smiled,
As if remembering something pleasant,
A friend's face or the gesture of a child.
A silver thing glittered in her hand;
It fascinated her; she tossed it back and forth
Then laughed and hid it playfully.
Then again she stared, head down,
Eyes blank, hand dully opened.

ELEANOR BARNES.

GREEN JANUARY

Warm, spring-like days that slip in quick succession
As in real gladness, to be free to leave
Dead trees, dry gardens, lifeless green-gray lawn,
Glad to give up the hopeless task at eve
To give place to another day at dawn.
And yet the air is trembling with repression;
Each gentle rainstorm comes and goes away
And seems to say, "If I could but control
The manner of my coming to the earth
I would not come in such a guise as this.

Great winds would trumpet, heralding my birth,
And clear my way, and bring me from the West.
I'd hold your woods and pastures to my breast,
Dry trees nor long bare hills shall bar my way.
Each twig, each vine, each tiny blade of grass
I'll in my pity clothe with icy sheaves.

Each naked tree that shivers where I pass
Shall be consoled for all its long lost leaves.
Proud birches I will bend, I'll hold them there
With ice, and they'll not laugh, for they'll not dare."
So spake the gentle rain of its suppression;
Again it said, "If I could but control
The manner of my coming down to you
I would not come in such a guise as this:
But greater powers than mine deny me bliss."
And so it rained, and no one heard but me,
Who always knew that rainstorms had a soul.
Who knew it just as sure had I not seen
The tracery of raindrops on the screen,
Mute evidence of hidden artistry,
And of well-hidden longing, mute confession.

                              KATHARINE KOSMAK.

THE EGOTIST IN HIS ORCHARD

I

The moon will rise and you will brood
Upon her dying solitude,
With every little wizened star
Reminding you how small we are.

II

Oh! what strange fruit is in my trees
To call the phosphorescent bees,
That they should leave their hives to come
And suck my one prodigious plum?

TOM PRIDEAUX.

SOME AND OTHERS AT THE PRIVATE VIEW

WHAT SOME SAW

Rough square houses;
Long-hewn beams, piled here and there;
Rat-trap jaws
On heavy-jowled foundations;
Lined ugliness.

WHAT OTHERS SAID

"Startling pictures!"
"Imaginative creations!"
"Inflorescence of the inner mind;
   Unattainable altitudes!"
"Cubic curves!"

PHILIP JORDAN.

QUASSIA WOOD

Oh, Vega is a distant star
Which blooms in firmaments afar.

And Vega sheds a pearly blue
(Perhaps that has a meaning too).

I think from Vega one could spy
Colors unknown to earthy eye:

Our mundane nose could never smell
Of Vega's spicy hydromel;

With normal palate we cannot
Attract ambrosial apricot . . .

It always seems that far away
The quassia trees are very few.
I wonder, is it really true?

                              ARTHUR BULLOWA.

FRENCH MINUET

PINK and blue—
                Pearl gown,
White-wigged
                Lady—
Stepping—swaying,
                Dancing tunes.

Cast a star-glance,
                White-wigged lady,
At milord's bronze
                Buckled shoe.
O, make love
                To-night—this once;
It matters not in
                Pink and blue.

Figure cut
            In satin stuff,
Just a pomp of lace,
Kisses silvered in the night
Blow upon his grace.

  Drop a curtsey
            Love, my love,
  Curtsey just by chance—
  Watch him bob his powdered cue,
            Bobbing it to you—to you?
  No, but to the dance!

                    BEATRICE WADHAMS.

THE SUN-SHUNNER

TRICKLING down from branch to branch
Like a saffron avalanche,

Filtering through the sylvan gauze
As a frozen topaz thaws,

Lay, in puddles on the moss,
Golden solar, apple-sauce.

"Strain the brilliance," I beseeched,
"Or my reason will be bleached!"

                    TOM PRIDEAUX.

FIREWORKS

SILVER FOUNTAINS

EXPLOSION in a jewel case!
  Trinkets, gems,
  Diadems,
Filigree like burning lace.

Watching all the baubles mount
  Always I
  Wonder why
They do not tinkle in their fount.

ROCKETS

A genie's arm, and sleeved in gold
Was thrust across the sky.   Behold,
How from his smoking palm there falls
A silent chime of colored balls.

TOM PRIDEAUX.

DECEMBER

A LITTLE boy stood on the corner
And shoveled bits of dirty, soggy snow
Into the sewer—
With a jagged piece of tin.

He was helping spring come.

SANDERSON VANDERBILT.

NATURE NOTES

THE HAPPY HYENA

WHY does the gay hyena laugh?
Is he endeavoring to chaff,
Or does he want us all to see
How *very* genial he can be?
Or giving us an exhibition
Of his remarkable dentition?

THE WILD HOME-PUSSY

I love little pussy, her coat is so warm,
But when she grows vocal she loses her charm.
Her sphere is not the concert stage;
She should know better at her age.

Our very nicest cats don't roam;
A pussy's place is in the home
Purring, and being there to pat.
She should confine herself to that,
Never competing for the honors
Bestowed on human prima donnas.

THE WISE WOOD-PUSSY

The pensive polecat is not shy;
Perhaps that is the reason why
He has no popularity.

I wonder, does he e'er observe
That people, when they meet him, swerve
In a wide, rudely pointed curve.

It does not seem to cause him woe;
He simply smiles, and in a glow
Of victory, retires slow.

EMMA ROUNDS.

TO JULIA, CAUTIONING HER AGAINST INFECTIOUS DISEASES

WHEN as with measles Julia goes
She's colored like a red, red rose,
Even unto her dainty nose.
Next, when she's taken with the mumps
Her cheeks are but unsightly lumps—
Then how my admiration slumps!

EMMA ROUNDS.

THE CIRCUS

THE PARADE

HERE it comes with all its clamor,
All its grand and gaudy glamour,

Tell me when such spangled wonder was displayed?
All of Solomon's possessions
And the emperor's processions
　Never rivaled half the pomp of this parade.

See the harem maids Circassian
Garbed in Oriental fashion
　From the earrings to the henna on their feet,
In the gilded howdahs swaying
And majestically surveying
　All the awed and gaping people in the street.

See the herds of jeweled dragons
Coiling over crimson wagons,
　Watch the unicorns a-whirling on the wheels!
And the fat and portly cherubs
Sailing under scarlet scarabs,
　Who are fleeing for their lives from copper eels.

THE SIDE-SHOW

Tremendous!   Stupendous!
Zaboo, the giant!
Joz, the magician!
Lynn, death-defiant!
Ten cents admission!

THE MENAGERIE

Wistful lions' eyes behind bright cages
Lit with tolerance like martyred sages.
Hippopotamuses dream of sprawling
Where a river thick with ooze is crawling.
Slim giraffes display their mottled graces,
Longing for a desert's cool oasis.
Monkeys screech in panic as if mocking
Chewing-gum posterity for gawking.

THE BIG SHOW

Troupes of boisterous strutting clowns
   With yellow cheeks and painted grins,
A far cry from the love-sick frowns
   Of sad pierrots and harlequins.

Careening through the polished paraphernalia
   Like birds among the jungles of a dream,
The acrobats in glittering regalia
   Dazzle life with their own sequin's gleam.

Then bowing when their lauded act is ended,
   And tossing kisses, jaunty and so glib,
I wonder if they really comprehended
   They've tickled Death along his bony rib?

TOM PRIDEAUX.

THE MORON TURNS

OR

THE DANGER OF FOLLOWING THE PHILOSOPHER WHO SAID, "KNOW THYSELF."

I

At Intelligence Tests
I am not at my best,
They are not my idea of a spree;
They possess no attractions for me.
   There is no fascination
   Or fervid elation
   In slowly and patient-
Ly filling the blanks
That confront me in ranks.
   There are other, better ways,
   Of passing idle days

Than eternally perusing
A hazily confusioning
Ultimately disillusioning
 Test.
  And the rest,
The things the tests show,
I'd much rather not know.

II

It dwelt among untrodden ways,
 Obscure, unknown to fame,
An I. Q. nobody could raise
 But nobody could blame.
It dwelt apart, and few could know
 'Twas low as low could be;
Until I took a test—then, oh!
 The difference to me!

EMMA ROUNDS.

TROPICS

I

SEE the cockatoos' vermilion,
Watch the monkey's mad cotillion,
 Swaying in the coconut trees.
Listen to their giddy gibber . . .
 Have you known a jabber glibber
 Have you heard birds babble as these?

An old baboon all day absorbs
 Himself in efforts vain to make
 His eyelids stretch, although they ache,
To cover up protruding orbs.

II

Hear the cannibal hum,
    And dance,
    With lance,
And beat his drum.

On his head a waving cluster
Like a giant feather duster
Shades the oiled and umber luster
    Of his body from the sun.
As he wails of heathen cults, his
Throbbing diaphragm convulses
And the soul within him pulses
    As the magic rite is done.

From a flame hibiscus plant
Crouching women watch him rant.
Eyes of wonder overawed
By the jungle's gloom and gaud,
By the sea's eternal din,
By a shark-toothed idol's grin.
By the fear that death may be
On that idol's steaming knee.

III

The sun slips down;
Listless palm fronds flap;
    The foam-fringed,
    Sun-singed,
    Flame-tinged
Waves lap, lap.

                                TOM PRIDEAUX.

MORAL TALES

MARY AND BETTY

MARY, at the soda fountain,
Ate a promising young mountain
Of candy, sodas, and ice cream—
Made the drug-store man just beam—
Staggered home an awful mess,
With chocolate on her nice new dress.
Mother, cross, gave darling daughter
For supper, butter, bread, and water.

Betty, who lived right next door,
Was a virtuous little bore
Who disdained a druggist's store.
On the night of Mary's spree
Her mamma gave her for her tea
What she always gave her daughter—
Healthful butter, bread, and water.

There's a moral somewhere here—
Find it for yourself, my dear.

MABEL

Mabel is so good and sweet;
Keeps everything so nice and neat;
Does exactly what she should—
Mabel's very, very good.
Sometimes a little idea strikes her—
Isn't it queer that no one likes her?

JOHNNY

Johnny used to find content
In standing always rather bent,
Like an inverted letter J.
His angry relatives would say,

"Stand up! don't slouch! You've got a spine,
Stand like a lamp-post, not a vine!"
One day they heard an awful crack—
He'd stood up straight—it broke his back!

EMMA ROUNDS.

ON MY LADY'S FINGERNAIL

OH, MOST exquisite, many-tinted oval
Tipping the digit of my fair Hortense,
When once before thee, I can only grovel,
Indifference is but obvious pretence.
A tiny crescent forms a milky curve
Like the plump bosom of a cooing dove,
Setting a-tingle each and every nerve
Awaking dormant fires of passionate love.

Ten glistening tear-drops from my fingers drip
Teetering precariously from thy quivering brinks,
While love-lorn I can only stand and sip
In trembling haste ten eager, thirsty drinks.
But, sweetest Lady, though I would not carp,
I find thy nails, forsooth, a trifle sharp.

HOPE SPINGARN.

URBAN TRANSPORTATION SONGS

THE SUBWAY

CHILDREN, see this pretty thing,
Every morning it will bring
Loads of people to the city.
Isn't it an awful pity
That they have to stand and swing
By a silly little string
Precariously balancing?

If mayhap they get a seat
Someone stands upon their feet;
If they keep their elevation
By employing concentration,
In their fervid exultation
They are sure to pass their station!

THE BALLAD OF THE MERRY FERRY

Sing hey and sing ho and sing down-a-down-derry,
Oh, what is so merry
As missing the ferry!

A nice wintry morning
So jolly and freezing
A dear little cold keeps you coughing and sneezing
And everyone mirthful and happy and gay
As we all watch the ferry go puffing away.

Sing hey and sing ho and sing down-a-down-derry,
Oh, what is so merry
As missing the ferry!

EMMA ROUNDS.

HE DID!

He WALKED and walked and walked
    And then? He walked some more
Till he arrived at length
    At the country store.

He bought and bought and bought,
    And then? He bought some more
And when he'd finished buying
    There was naught in the store.

He walked and walked and walked,
  And then? He walked some more
Until he came at length
  To his own front door.

He pulled and pulled and pulled,
  And then? He pulled some more
Until he pulled the hinges
  Off his own front door.

He walked and walked and walked,
  And then? He walked some more
Until he landed breathless
  On his bedroom floor.

                    PAULINE BAERWALD.

MOON

WITHERED wanton of the night,
  Draw the clouds about your face;
Harsher stuff is all for youth,
  Age sedately sanctions lace.

                    TOM PRIDEAUX.

OUT THERE

THE other night a fellow left, and
He was a real friend of mine
And sometimes at night, when
I'm thinking about things,
I wonder where he's gone,
And if he's coming back,
And what it's like out there.

                    STEPHEN DUGGAN.

THE BEAUTY OF HER

THE beauty of her lies not in her smile
But in the petulant droop of her lips;
Not in the gleam of her smooth curls,
But in that one vagrant lock which has escaped.

Not in her silken gown sh'mmering in the light,
But in the snubbed toe of her little slipper;
Not in the gentle love shining from her eyes,
But in the sly glance of mischief which I caught unawares.

ALICE HABBERTON.

TANG

HE LIKED peaches—
They were soft and sweet.

A green persimmon
Was her delight:
It left her mouth all puckered.

ZORA HEAD.

SEASONAL IMPRESSIONS

I HAVE experienced
The languorous haze
Of a summer eve,
And the crackling cold
Of a winter morn;
And I have felt
The tired mist
Of an autumn noon;
And the sparkling wine
Of a youthful spring.

LINCOLN REIS.

KIN

I switched the light off;
And as I turned
To shield myself
From the keen night air
I heard the swishing
Of the trees
Trying on *their* new
Spring dresses.

ELLA FOHS.

THE NORTH WIND

A Shivering Song

I

The North Wind shakes the shivering moon
And rattles the windows with a banging tune
Hurling his message at the earth
And hugging the trees with a shout of mirth.

II

Howling his challenge to the night
With all his blustering windy might
The North Wind clings to his hard-won prize
With a mist-wreath'd brow and starlit eyes.

LINCOLN REIS.

THE LAND OF THINGS FORGOTTEN

A pale, slender shot of silver from the moon
Came through my window last night before dawn,
And struck the dark oval mirror with white.
It shone back with an empty gleam,
Making a pale, pale-white gold daffodil
Standing in a copper vase on a dark polished table,
Paler and more graceful still.

As the stars that shone silently in the dark failed,
So did the weird, uncanny black night—
And the dead, gray, quiet dawn crept in.

The moonbeam and the daffodil faded.
The silent, ghostly shadows of black and gray disappeared,
And the host of dreams and imaginings
Which people my room at night
Went to the land of things forgotten, where some day
I shall find them;
And the moon-beam and the daffodil,
When I go there too.

ANNE PAPPENHEIMER.

THE CALL OF THE AIR

A MAN who stands by his cottage door,
   Gazing over the ocean wild and free,
A wish to discover lures within,
   This is the call of the sea!

A man who sees beyond the hills,
   Who sees a waste of stretching sand,
Then sees the fruits of Nature there,
   This is the call of the land!

A man who sleeps beneath the stars,
   And into the depth of space can stare,
A man who sees beyond the world,
   This is the call of the air!

GHOLSON KITTREDGE.

TIRED WATER

I HEAR it
Playing on the roof,
    In April;
With a soft, sweet sound.

I hear it,
Jumping down the rocks
Like silver
With a long glad bound.

I hear it,
The swelling tossing ocean
    In March,
Showing its fangs with a roar.

Rearing,
In a high blue ridge,
White capped,
And beating on the shore.

The brook
So wise and so silly
So musical
Like cold crystal—at home.

Tired water,
Enslaved by man to work
In mills,
Struggling for freedom, cannot roam.

                    ANNE PAPPENHEIMER.

TINSEL

Where is Tinsel?

Out in the rain
Singing a ditty
And crying . . .

Look in the puddles
The lights that are there
Poppy . . . Poppy
Lilac and gold,
So many faëries
Wingless and cold.
So many faëries
Shut out of the skies,
Because they grew old,
And foolishly wise . . .

Beatrice Wadhams.

CAVALIER'S DITTY

When my father was young, he roamed over the earth,
With a heart like a feather, a soul full of mirth,
And he made him a vow on the night of my birth,
To make me a soldier of fortune.

A soldier of fortune was I, was I,
As carefree as ever a lark in the sky,
Tho older and wiser in scorn passed me by,
For I was a soldier of fortune.

I roamed thru each village and town, every town,
But my purse remained empty—I won no renown,
And the fates laughed in triumph to see me cast down,
For I was a soldier of fortune.

When I saw that my efforts would nothing avail,
I wondered that ever I'd follow the trail
And squandered the days of my youth—but to fail,
  For I was a soldier of fortune.

But a richer reward than mere gold did I earn,
And a maid taught me that which I yet had to learn,
So that now I've a haven to which I can turn,
  For I'm no more a soldier of fortune.

                                    ALINE WECHSLER.

SEA-GODS

GIANTS
Powerful . . . wet
Slapping the sandy beach . . .

When do you sleep?

                                    WILMA ROELOFSMA.

AKIB, KING OF EGYPT'S SON

AKIB, king of Egypt's son
Lay by the river Do Dum Dun,
Lay on the gray-green sands
Of Egypt land,
On Egypt's gray-green sand.

Lay beneath the oily palm,
Humming a song to the Ukeadahm
Till he fell asleep, in the middle of June,
Singing away to the crocodile's tune,
To the tune of the ugly crocodile,
As it beat its tail in the river Nile;
Tum . . . tum . . . tum
On the back of a hollow bamboo drum.

As he lay asleep beneath the palm,
He dreamt he saw the Ukeadahm
Come step by step o'er the gray-green sand,
O'er the gray-green sand of Egypt land,
With stealthy steps, with cautious looks,
Washing his face in the cool of the brooks,
In the brooks
That wound about through sheltered nooks.

Through the sheltered nooks of Egypt land
That haunt the fields of gray-green sand
Came the Ukeadahm with his heavy trod
Crushing the soil and mashing the sod
Spoiling the sands of Egypt land,
As he sifted the grains through his hoof-like hand,
Sifting the grains
To the wind that blew over Egypt land.

Akib dreamt that the moon broke out
In the sky above him, and tossed about
Like a ship on the sea, in the trough of a storm,
Fighting the waves as the night went on;
And he saw the moon shiver at the crocodile
As it thumped its tail in the river Nile,
Tum . . . tum . . . tum
On the back of a hollow bamboo drum.

On and on came the Ukeadahm,
Till he looked and saw the oily palm
And Akib lying on the gray-green sand,
The gray-green sands of Egypt land,
And heard the ugly crocodile
As it beat its tail in the river Nile,
Tum . . . tum . . . tum
On the back of a hollow bamboo drum.

And the dew came down on the oily palm
And wet the gruesome Ukeadahm
And formed a mist of muggy white,
That glistened through the pale moonlight,
And fell in drops on the gray-green sand,
And moistened
Drop by drop, Egypt's gray-green sand.

And the mist enshrouded the Ukeadahm
Enshrouded the Nile and the oily palm,
Covered Egypt's gray-green sand,
The gray-green sands of Egypt land,
Enveloped the river Do Dum Dun,
And Akib, king of Egypt's son,
And the crocodile
As he beat with his tail in the river Nile.

And Akib woke beneath the palm,
Woke from his dream of the Ukeadahm,
Covered with dew from the mist all around,
As he lay on the gray-green sandy ground,
Woke to the tune of the crocodile
As he beat with his tail in the river Nile,
Tum . . . tum . . . tum
On the back of a hollow bamboo drum.

SAMUEL LYNCH.

RAIN–RIDING

DRENCHED, soaked, sopped
I sat on top of a bus;
No one else had climbed the stairs.
The rain was splashing down;
I huddled under a half broken umbrella . . .
Two dull lights showed dimly through the haze
From a ship on the river.

MARY RUMELY.

SONG

MANDARIN, Mandarin
  Nod your head!
My heart is a moonstone
  Cold and dead,
Mandarin . . .
Nod!

One love of mine
  They killed by scorn;
Another love . . .
  Died of itself
But the third
  Was the first
That taught me to hate . . .
And that was the love
  That came too late

Mandarin! Mandarin!
  Say it was fate . . .
Mandarin
Nod.

BEATRICE WADHAMS.

O SAILORS!

HERE upon the rocks we lie,
  And gaze in scorn up to the sun,
  For, self-sufficient, fear we none;
And idly watch the ships pass by.

Ah, idly? Who that word shall say
  Concerning us! Have not the waves
  Taken unto themselves the graves
We made, while seeming but to play?

Ye sailors! Hither, one and all.
   Come, join our gambols here the while,
   For we will time and thoughts beguile.
Can one of you resist our call?

The reefs o'er yon are but a prank
   Some wanton Fate has played your eyes;
   Come, enter into Paradise!
Who fears to touch upon this bank?

O sailors! Hear our voices low,
   Would you not come and closer be
   That you may all this beauty see,
To rest with us, and never go?

ALINE WECHSLER.

LULLABY

LET the shooting stars
   Play tag
Chase the wind—or follow
   The moon;
Let the lone ships toss
   Like leaves,
To the ocean's frantic tune.

Through the tireless night
   You sleep
Hushed by the silent sky
   To the silver slumber
Of a fairy's lullaby.

PRISCILLA WADHAMS.

THE BLACKFEET OF MONTANA

I MET the chiefs in the morning, (and oh, but I am old!)
Where roaring down the canyon the summer west wind
   rolled.

I heard them lift the war-whoop that quelled the gray-wolf's
   song,
The Blackfeet of Montana—two thousand voices strong!

The cry of warring nations along Montana's plain,
The whoop of scalping squadrons that stripped the bleeding
   slain,
The chant of frenzied dances that churned the heart to flame—
The Blackfeet of Montana—before the pale-face came!

I met the braves in the morning (I'll meet them ne'er again);
They came and went in parties that dotted all the plain.
And as the pioneers came west, their squatter homes to make,
We slew the scattered vanguard, and burned them at the
   stake!

The plains of old Montana—the badland buttes so tall,
The great-browed red-eyed bison, the flint-clawed pumas call,
The game-trails of our hunting grounds, all shining smooth and
   worn!
The plains of old Montana—the home where we were born!

The Blackfeet met in the morning, a broken, scattered band,
The white men shoot us down like dogs, to rob us of our land.
They drive us from our homeland, broken and cowed and
   tame;
But we recall Montana before the pale-face came!

Wheel out, wheel out to the eastward; oh, prairie falcon, go!
And tell the eastern nations the story of our woe;
Ere, empty as the clam-shell the river flings ashore,
The plains of old Montana shall know their sons no more.
WILLIAM SARGENT.

SOME DAY, MAYBE

BENEATH the magic Cherry Tree,
Beside the Stone of Mystery
 Where fairies play,

A sort of mist is over there,
But birds will call and lead you where
 The fairies play.

Some day maybe you will see
The Tree and Stone of Mystery
 Where fairies play.

PRISCILLA WADHAMS.

OH, FISHMAN, SWEET FISHMAN

"OH, FISHMAN, sweet Fishman, where do you get your fish?
 For you know the sea's a thousand miles away."
"When it rains," he said, "in torrents I catch them in a dish,
 Or a teaspoon, or a jar-top, or a tray.

"Then I put them in the bathtub, which they always do en-
 joy
 As it's purple trimmed with violet all around,
And I feed them sour fishworms, and a certain sweet alloy
 Procured by placing mouse-traps underground.

"The sunfish get excited and squirm between the rails,
 But I feed the infant oysters with a spoon,
And if the trout are lonesome, and the baby catfish wails,
 I play with them until it's half-past noon."

JOHN CROLY.

NEW YEARS

LIKE a new-burst bud
Twelve petals all
Open one by one,
Fade, and then fall;
So, very like buds
Yet unfurled,
Lie the future years
Hiddenly curled.

SUSAN KRONTHAL.

MORNING

TWIGS crackle frostily in the cold blue light of morning;
Hazy smoke from kitchen fires while light is dawning;
Mountain peaks are misty in the yellow morning sun,
And many a dog is barking that the day's work is begun.

NATHALIE SWAN.

PITEOUS EYES

A STATELY figure pacing ever
To and fro, to and fro,
His tawny well-brushed coat
Of mellow walnut stain,
Darkened here and there,
Was beautiful;
    His majestic air was
Startling
    But for his piteous eyes
Piercing his one line of vision,
    The walls of his captivity.

MARY SPURRIER.

THE BARN-SWALLOW

In the Alleghany mountains
  When the apple orchards bloom
I know of eaves in a big red barn
  Where I'll find nesting room

I'm coming back! I'm coming back!
  My wings are on the wind;
I'm coming back with the spring-time
  To the hills I've left behind

I'm coming back! I'm coming back
  To the hills that I know best,
Where the mountains sleep, and the winds walk
  And where my wings can rest

In the Alleghany mountains
  When the apple orchards bloom
I know of eaves in a big red barn
  Where I'll find nesting room.

WILLIAM SARGENT.

BIZARRE

This is the season of the frost,
Of the silver and the white
That come in the night,
Of the mornings clear and cold
When the sun pours down white gold,
Lifting the cobweb veil from off the green.

This is the season of bizarre,
Of the red and the gold,
Color-glories untold,

When the hills are wearing blankets,
Where the orange has no limits
And the sky is full of rainbows chopped up small.

ANNE PAPPENHEIMER.

OUR LADY OF THE SHIPWRECKED

*(A statue, Notre Dame des Naufragés, on an exposed point of the
Breton coast.)*

WIND-LASHED and tempest-worn, above the sea
  She stands, in mourning robes of sullen skies,
  And on her back, a people's burden lies,
And in her ears, there rings a people's plea:

"Bring back our fathers from the gloating waves!
  Oh take our sailor kinsmen by the hand
  And lead them through the fog and storm to land!
Great Mother, raise our people from their graves!"

The wind calls to the sea,
And the sea
Sweeps her robes about her dead
In melody.

ELEANOR FLEXNER.

PEOPLE

THE length of shooting stars
  They live, and wonder why;
Then rearrange their earthly beds
  And settle down to die.

PHILIP JORDAN.

WE MEET AGAIN

Wɪᴛʜ half a laugh of hearty zest
I strip me of my coat and vest.

Then, heeding not the frigid air,
I fling away my underwear,

So, having nothing else to doff,
I rip my epidermis off.

More secrets to acquaint you with,
I pare my bones to strips of pith

And when the exposé is done
I hang, a cobweb skeleton. . . .

While there you sit, aloof, remote,
And will not shed your overcoat.

Tom Prideaux.

ANCHORITE

Tɪᴍᴇ is elusive;
I do not waste it
toiling to aid and serve
a thankless universe.

But, as a heedless Nero,
oblivious to all,
I play my squeaky fiddle in a
burning world.

Sanderson Vanderbilt.

ON CERTAIN POETS

AMY LOWELL

When I bring you a peony,
Torn, and trampled on by the rain,
You shake off the soil and put it
In a crystal vase,
Because you know—
Don't you?

When I bring you a poem
Written with my heart's blood,
A poem people cannot understand
Because it was not written for them—or by them,
You lay it quietly on the flames
And let it fly away in gray smoke
Because you understand—
Don't you?

When I bring you my soul,
Disregarded, forgotten
By all but me—and perhaps you—
You tell me that in these days
A soul is unnecessary—useless—
And you smile,
Because you are—you,
Aren't you?

JOHN MASEFIELD

Let not the forests shorten your sight
Like an arrow stopped by a tree;
Let not the hills cut off with their height
The place where your gaze should be;
But follow the sea gull's scopeless flight

And the outward stretch of the sea.
Unreachable storm clouds that come at night,
The waves, outbound by the new moon's light,
And the water gardens, sunless yet bright,
Are the hills and the trees of the sea.

CARL SANDBURG

LISTEN to me.   You are all making a mistake;
You don't know beauty when you see it.
There is beauty in the tangle of gas pipes under a city street;
The empty lots at the city's edge are beautiful;
And there is really poetry in the heap of tin cans beside a
    suburban brook.

Listen to me.   You who try to let the glory of the sun at mid-
    day
Blind your eyes to these things;
You fool yourselves into thinking that the pale dawn hides
    them;
You weep because there is a pumpkin vine growing in the
    dump heap.
You don't understand.
I don't expect you to.
Beauty is a custom like everything else.

SARA TEASDALE

ALL that is bitter and all that is sweet,
    Lord, you have given me to taste;
All of your problems I tried to meet;
    Now have your bounteous gifts gone to waste?

Joy have I felt, and love and hate,
    Pain and envy and ecstasy,
Failure, success, and the hand of fate,
    All have you caused to be laid on me.

Now I have mixed them and have placed
   All my life at your patient feet;
Lord, you have given me all to taste;
   Which is bitter and which is sweet?

WILLIAM ROSE BENÉT

OUR mission in this world consists of three
Great underlying tasks: one is to fight
To keep the world from crushing in its flight
The kind of person that you want to be.

The second task seems small—infinitely:
To fill the moment when we are in sight
With light—with all that we can give of light
To make our children see—and want to see.

The third task is, down in your heart to know—
Still being sure you are not really wise—
That all the suns and stars that flame and glow,
Those swooping, whirling things, are Someone's eyes
That watch you, with the power to overthrow
Your star, and send you crashing through the skies.

EDNA ST. VINCENT MILLAY

THE world came by and tugged at my wrist;
I laughed, and it ran away with me
Over a wide sea of jade and of amethyst,
Through deep cool forests, soft-packed with the summer mist.
Joyously, all last week, I let it play with me.

This week has brought me much work to complete;
Pen, broom, and book shall spend all of each day with me;
Many neglected tasks clutch at my feet.
When the world comes to me, calling so sweet,
Will I resist it?—oh, human deceit—
Joyously, all this week, I'll let it play with me!

KATHARINE KOSMAK.

COQUETTE

THIS dulled moth startles you?
   It will confound you more
When to-morrow I
Return to butterfly.
I'll turn my fickle head
As I take leave
And watch you brush
   My wings' dust-powder
From your sleeve.

ZORA HEAD.

SOPHOMORE

LEAVE me
   For I am busy
   I am tired of doing
Things in firm staid ways
Away!—
I must absorb myself in doing
   Nothing.

ZORA HEAD.

AT KENILWORTH

"THIS stately edifice of storied stone—
Ancient adornments of high heraldry;
My own best council, modest—as you see;
All that I have and am shall be thine own.
My very heart lies open at thy throne,
And all my highest hope shall ever be
To kneel in endless fealty to thee—
Great mistress, and to worship thee alone."

So spoke false Leicester to the wary queen
Whose upraised hand might chasten or endow
With equal power.   When did that subtle smile
Ever give hope to him who would beguile?
Yet for one moment flushed her woman's brow;
In that shrewd eye, an unshed tear was seen.

LOUISE LAIDLAW.

THOSE THINGS THAT ONCE HAVE BROUGHT US HAPPINESS

THOSE things that once have brought us happiness
   We wish to keep, to give us joy once more;
   The ecstasy which we have felt before
We would bring back, our future hours to bless.

And so we build a shrine and worship there,
   Or learn by rote the thoughts we wish to feel;
   In some remembrancer we try to seal
The essence that once made our fancies fair.

But joy is uncontrolled as is a stream
   That sparkles, scintillating in its haste,
     Yet ceases when no longer flow the springs;
Likewise the beauty of a tender dream
   Will fade away, unless we newly taste
     The holy, sweet elation that love brings.

ARTHUR E. BESTOR, JR.

THE GALLEY-PROOF OF THE POETIC PUDDING

MUCH have I traveled in the realms of wit,
Full many goodly jests and verses read;
Through pages crammed with humor have I sped
And smiled in passing at some subtle hit.

Oft, reading stuff that brighter minds had writ
A vague ambition in my soul was bred,
I, even I, could, so I vainly said,
Be funnier than that—till I tried it.

Then felt I like some watcher of the skies
When on a picnic he sees coming rain;
Or like a student bard, whose anguished eyes
Stare at the precious products of his brain,
Censored, blue-penciled, scoffed at by the wise,
Upon a heap of literary slain.

EMMA ROUNDS.

PLANE GEOMETRY

'TWAS Euclid, and the theorem pi
  Did plane and solid in the text,
All parallel were the radii,
  And the ang-gulls convex'd.

"Beware the Wenworth-Smith, my son,
  And the Loci that vacillate;
Beware the Axiom, and shun
  The faithless Postulate."

He took his Waterman in hand;
  Long time the proper proof he sought;
Then rested he by the XYZ
  And sat awhile in thought.

And as in inverse thought he sat
  A brilliant proof, in lines of flame,
All neat and trim, it came to him,
  Tangenting as it came.

"AB, CD," reflected he—
  The Waterman went snicker-snack—
He Q.E.D.-ed, and, proud indeed,
  He trapezoided back.

"And hast thou proved the 29th?
  Come to my arms, my radius boy!
O good for you!   O one point two!"
  He rhombussed in his joy.

'Twas Euclid, and the theorim pi
  Did plane and solid in the text;
All parallel were the radii
  And the ang-gulls convex'd.

EMMA ROUNDS.

HONORS

ALAS, I looked on lands too far,
  Reached out beyond my place,
And now I sing the treble bar
  While others play the bass.

PHILIP JORDAN.

WALT WHITMAN

I

WALT WHITMAN, you enigma,
You egotist, who flaunt yourself
Naked to the world,
You many-sided one.
You preacher of beauty
In halting lines
That sweep one before their flood
And bore one to death.

Walt Whitman, you pain me,
I am tortured when I read you;
But I read you.

You preach physical strength
The physical roughness and strength of
Freeborn man.
You, who nursed the wounded more gently
Than the gentlest woman,
Walt Whitman, it is only you who can do that.

You cannot please me
Like some minor poet
Of candied prettiness,
Who is to you
Like some sweet, shrubbed hill
To some gigantic mountain.
Walt Whitman, you bore me, I am sick of you;
I hate your conceits and affectations—
And your nakedness.
You tire me to death;
But I will come back to you.

LINCOLN REIS.

JAZZ, TINTER OF SOULS

INVOCATION

JAZZ, universally scoffed at, deplored by the older generation, horrifying the purists, we float through space, swung
upward by your billows, swinging with your undulations,
made light by the spell of your syncopation.

Jazz, how many mechanical hearts have you pulsed with
the vivid throb of life, how many feet have you lifted, how
many souls have you momentarily raised from their drabness
with the spell of your syncopation?

Jazz, you have fostered many dreams with the cadence of

your wistful waltzes and the rapid heat of your fox-trots; many eyes have seen before them glimmering futures while you beat through their veins with the spell of your syncopation.

Jazz, how often have you misted the glaring night with romance, how often have minds been filled with chivalrous fire, with self-told tales of valor in the cause of romance by the spell of your syncopation.

Jazz, tinter of souls, we recognize your imperfections, yet we bow before the spell of your syncopation.

II

IMPRESSION

RIPPLE of beats; pounding hard on that one; gentle under-swing of a cloak that swishes; basic frivolity that will not calm; alluring twists stick out on top; hear it curl! A crimson slide; a greased pole with rectangular bumps; bruises that rub one the right way; underneath the grumbling of an old man, an old man that enjoys grumbling! "The World is Waiting for the Sunrise"; a bang with fraying edges rounding a curve at full speed only to find the other side like the one before; starched laces becoming soft in contact with the throat! A yodel with a turned-up nose; out from below the cliff the pulsing cataract, yet it doesn't even ripple! Green leap-frog; a moon with three wisps of cloud; "California, Here I Come"!; Yan, yan Yah-ha-ha! A speck against the sky; a majestic sun leaping like a frog; a pool with darting fish over gleaming mud!

III

YOUNG WHILE THE WORLD IS OLD

WE TALKED and some joke I made
Set you laughing, then I was pleased
That you should think me witty,
And all the while the jazz band played
Some pounding leaping tune. You sneezed;
I said it was a pity

That you should have a cold. You smiled;
It hadn't killed you yet, you said;
I quite agreed, seeing you weren't dead.
You smiled again and asked if I
Knew your dear pal, old Betty Wild.
I didn't. The sax began again to cry.
"What's that they're playing now? You know it?
What is the name? Forgotten? Oh, blow it!
It doesn't make any difference anyway.
It's jolly though! Let's dance! What say?"

IV

ATMOSPHERE

THE jazz band plays a lisping tune
And the sax's cry turns the air maroon,
And the stars above must dance with the moon
And the clouds must swing in time,
For none can resist the jazzy air
And the pulses beat to the sax's blare,
And the swinging head of the banjo player
With his plucking strings' thin chime.

The polished floor is a rippling lake
And the mirrored lights are the moon's bright wake
Though the dancing feet like gulls' wings make
A reiterated whirr.
And the hair is held by a diadem,
And the shoe made fast by a flaring gem,
And they twinkle like rain on a sun-drenched stem
When the wind makes the spectra stir.

The dancers move for the moment's end;
They have no hope they must ascend,
No gripping cloud that they must rend

And find the peak still far;
For the moment's swing is the moment's joy,
And to-morrow's prick cannot annoy
The lilting girl and the laughing boy,
And the music's pulsed huzzar.

A song is sung by the flying feet,
A song of life, bright, rounded, fleet,
Where no gray end of drab can meet
The impetuous and blind,
And——
                                    JAMES FLEXNER.

LINCOLN

WE COULD not use a meaning word,
Or find a fitting sacrifice,
That would ring true, if he had heard,
Who saved us with so high a price.
The greater tribute paid instead,
We, silent, left our thoughts unsaid.
                                    ALINE WECHSLER.

CONTENT ON A BUS

I CAN imagine you
Going home through the spring dusk
In the blended harmony
Of distant city sounds;
And the bus will jerk and rock,
But you will see
Only the first star,
Gold in a green sky;
And you will be warm,
Warm with the happiness
That would be mine—
Were I there.
                                    ZARA MOXHAM.

LANTERNS

OH, SMOKY lantern, with your unwashed chimney
As you sway in halting rhythm
To the jolting of the wagon
In your lonely, rocking darkness of the night!

SANDERSON VANDERBILT.

CHRISTMAS AFTER THANKSGIVING

THINE is a tree to deck, Lord, to whom thanks we raise,
Branches that, quivering, stretch full of hope to Thee.
Yesterday breaking hearts sang loud thy name to praise,
Counting the little joys, filling their empty days,
Prayed that their thanks to Thee might truly grateful be.

Thine is a tree to deck, Lord, who for many lands
Mixed love with burning hate, gave joy to still the pain.
For those few golden threads, woven through iron strands,
They will love life anew, steady their trembling hands.
Now they have felt the pain; let the tree blaze again!

KATHARINE KOSMAK

WHEN I WAS VERY YOUNG

WHEN I was very young—and knew much more
Than I do now, a book clasped round with gold
Once made me wonder what things it could hold
So precious they must be locked behind a door.
I wondered, when I opened it, to see
Only two pictures, and the unknown words
Covering the pages like the tracks of birds
Who have paced out of sight majestically.

One picture showed a baby on the hay
And kings and shepherds kneeling on the ground
With angels singing, and a star on high
Shedding its light on where the baby lay.
Another, at the very end I found—
A man upon a cross against the sky.

KATHARINE KOSMAK.

EXPLANATIONS

WHEN the Sky weeps and the Clouds are in tears
   The Stars have a hard time.   Poor little dears!
They have to open their umbrellas wide—
   That's why we can't see them from the outside.

When the Gods get mad and start slamming about,
   The poor timid Moon is in terrible doubt,
She doesn't know whether to laugh or to cry,
   So she flings a black mantle all over the Sky.

When the Sun is angry and gets awfully hot,
   The Earth is just a Dried Up Spot;
It is parched and wrinkled and much too warm
   And would eagerly welcome a Hard Rain Storm.

But the dear little Stars and the poor timid Moon
   (To say nothing of the Dried Up Spot)
All feel happy when the Gods are good—
   And it's not too dreadfully hot.

NANCY DENNETT.

CONFESSIONAL

Two people passed through my woods to-day
And whispered to my dogwood tree
Fervently,
As if they loved to be
Looking at a tree.

He reached to pick a blossom
Then stuck it in her hair;
She stroked its pinkness
But left it there,
Too beautiful
To cast away
Yet too innocent
To stay,

Then spoke, low to the tree,
Loving its purity—
Fearful to look away
Lest she might betray
Her secret.

He mumbled words
Incoherent and wild
Talking to a dogwood
Like a child . . .

They turned away
Forgetting now the tree
Radiant-eyed
And free.

And I, too, went my way
Knowing it could not be.
Who ever heard of people
Speaking with a tree?

PHILIP JORDAN.

AH!

You think to forget me?
Good.
A pretty thought . . .

WILMA ROELOFSMA.

PATIENT

I SHALL leave it all to you;
Merely to have the pleasure
Of seeing your deft thin fingers
Make the paper gray.

It would be quite useless
For me to try to work
The spell that the enchantress Vivien
Gave to you.   It would be unfair—
As was she.

For though you are powerful,
Someday a divining soul
Will wreck some wonder on your mind.
I will not hurry the coming of that hour
Even though I may.

ELLA FOHS.

WELL!

You begged admittance
I said, "No,"
And closed the door.

A moment later
You climbed through the window
And sat down.

WILMA ROELOFSMA.

VITAL

FRIEND
When I am dust
Consider then our moments
Of rich friendship.

CHARLES LIEBMAN, JR.

SPRIG

I

DEEP-ROOTED stands
the smokestack
moored to its
grimy palace of
industry.
It will endure
for years
for it cannot appreciate
discontent.

II

Born of
a slave
the young smoke
inflated with
ambition
pursues the clouds.
It is new, powerful
and free—and—
is gone.

SANDERSON VANDERBILT.

SUCCOUR

WILL you
Who have a forest
Born of myriad suns,
Help me,
A fruitless wastrel
To plant my scentless yucca
By the sheen of tinsel stars?

ARTHUR BULLOWA.

A BALLAD OF LADY MOON

SMILE, Lady Moon, through your vapor of white,
Smile, though your beauty last only to-night,
Shadow the meadows with radiant light,
  Smile, Lady Moon.

Across the hills, now faintly gray,
There moves a mass of sheeted men,
Whose ghastly errand, ere the day,
Shall be repeated once again.

They hold a man, with stoic calm
And gallant smile he hides his care;
They bind him to a lone tree's arm,
And watch him, frantic, hopeless, there.

With Indian stealth and indrawn breath
They disappear behind a hill;
The figure, vanquished now by Death,
In weird contortion, hangs there . . . still.

Hide, Lady Moon, 'neath your sheathing of white,
Hide from all humans their fellow-man's plight,
Use as a curtain the jet of the night,
  Hide, Lady Moon.

ALINE WECHSLER.

THE HILLS

IF YOU are going to scold me
  For the little ills I do,
Scold me, and scold me quickly,
  For I am leaving you.

I'm leaving for my mountains
That lift their crests on high
Where I can climb their summits
And watch the eagles fly.

Upon the last long foothill's slope
I'll turn and wave and smile;
Then I'll forget among the hills,
And you may watch awhile.

WILLIAM SARGENT.

THE DARK HOURS OF THE NIGHT

WHEN I cross a stone-flagged alley
Of a little street hemmed in by two fences,
Save only where two doors lead back into my
Cell—
That is now to me, who have really lived,
My short moment of life.

I have loved the wind and the hills,
The sea breaking on white cliffs,
And I have laughed for
                            the joy of laughing,
Then next have cried,
                    because,
For a little, I was left out of beauty
And thrown into memory.
But now—all day long I stay in a house,
Or walk for one hour between long rows
Of stores
On a dead street
In a dead city

And I am like the others who
                            walk with me—

Feelingless.
I may not even cry.
(But I thank God that He
Has taken from me
The power to feel swift frightening pain;
I am left now with only the memory of hurt)
But, as a dream may come to life
During the dark hours of the night,
So for just the time
It takes to cross that little alley—
I may live.

ZARA MOXHAM.

FOOL

IN ONE black moment
I wrung life from my body
And gave it to you

You
You turned your head aside
To laugh.

WILMA ROELOFSMA.

QUEEN OF THE POND

Two swollen, distorted frogs
Squat beside the waterlily;
She holds them there on either side—
Two slow-blooded, pulseless beasts.
The gay bright-colored turtle she rejects,
She cares not for the lofty crane,
She spurns the rainbow-tinted sunfish.
All these
And more
This queen of flowers

Neglects.
Two swollen, distorted frogs
Lie there
Motionless and hideous . . .
Still.

SANDERSON VANDERBILT.

VENDETTA

To BLEED him slowly;
  With frozen words
Inserting in his open wound of penitence
  The venom
Of complete indifference;
Then not to care enough to watch him writhe.

ZORA HEAD.

WIND–WOLVES

Do YOU hear the cry as the pack goes by
The wind-wolves hunting across the sky?
Hear them tongue it, keen and clear,
Hot on the flanks of the flying deer?

Across the forest, mere, and plain,
Their hunting howl goes up again.
All night they'll follow the ghostly trail
All night we'll hear the phantom wail.

For to-night the wind-wolf pack holds sway
From Pegasus Square to the Milky Way
And the frightened bands of cloud deer flee
In scattered bands of two and three.

WILLIAM SARGENT.

NOW

I AM the Present.
I am the Everlasting Now.

I am the only thing that is alive.
I have seen all things that ever were,
But all of them died when I left.
Because I passed by, Cleopatra is rotting;
Alexander and Cæsar stopped their conquests when I left
    them;
As I walk away, empires crumble.
When I am gone, nothing can live;
Yet I will stop for no one.

Some day I will say good-bye to you,
And you will perish.

I carry with me the spoils of all the ages,
The ages which are dead because I am not with them.
I have stolen the fruits of everyone's labor to take along.
But I will not give them to you to keep.
Instead, I will despoil you
And carry the sum of all with me.

Wherever I go I will continue to pillage.
I do not know when I shall stop,
Any more than I know when I began.

When the Future comes, it will be I.

I am the Present.
I am the Everlasting Now.
                ARTHUR E. BESTOR, JR.

THE FOUR-MASTER

THEY say that you came from St. Joe
That you took three weeks to come
But I know
Where you are from.

They say that you carried white pine
Full to the poop-rail
Stacked on deck, line on line;
That you lost a studding sail.

But they are wrong:
I know
You came the Nebulæ along
And carry moon-snow

The sea you crossed
Was a far star's light
And the sail you lost
Was the wig of the night.

PHILIP JORDAN.

BEYOND

WHAT is more awful than a door?
Doors are opaque; one cannot see through them.
One can only hear, and imagine—and dread.

"Come," you say, "it is not so bad as that!"

But put your eye to the keyhole.
All you see is pressed in the mold of the keyhole;
Its shape leads you astray.